T

Simone Weil

1909–1943

Simone Weil

The Power of Words

Translated by Richard Rees and Arthur Wills

PENGUIN BOOKS — GREAT IDEAS

PENGUIN BOOKS

UK | USA | Canada | Ireland | Australia
India | New Zealand | South Africa

Penguin Books is part of the Penguin Random House group
of companies whose addresses can be found at
global.penguinrandomhouse.com.

Penguin
Random House
UK

'The Power of Words' and 'Human Personality' from
Selected Essays 1934–43 published 1962; 'The Needs of the Soul'
from *The Need for Roots* published 1962
Text taken from *Simone Weil: An Anthology*
published in Penguin Classics 2005
This selection first published in Penguin Books 2020
001

Copyright © Simone Weil, 1952, 1962
'The Needs of the Soul' translation copyright 1952 by Arthur Wills
'The Power of Words' and 'Human Personality'
translation copyright © Richard Rees, 1962

Set in 11.2/13.75 pt Dante MT Std
Typeset by Jouve (UK), Milton Keynes
Printed and bound in Great Britain by Clays Ltd, Elcograf S.p.A.

A CIP catalogue record for this book
is available from the British Library

ISBN: 978–0–241–47290–3

Contents

The Power of Words

The relative security we enjoy in this age, thanks to a technology which gives us a measure of control over nature, is more than cancelled out by the dangers of destruction and massacre in conflicts between groups of men. If the danger is grave it is no doubt partly because of the power of the destructive weapons supplied by our techniques; but these weapons do not fire themselves, and it is dishonest to blame inert matter for a situation in which the entire responsibility is our own. Common to all our most threatening troubles is one characteristic which might appear reassuring to a superficial eye, but which is in reality the great danger: *they are conflicts with no definable objective.* The whole of history bears witness that it is precisely such conflicts that are the most bitter. It may be that a clear recognition of this paradox is one of the keys to history; that it is the key to our own period there is no doubt.

In any struggle for a well-defined stake each combatant can weigh the value of the stake against the probable cost of the struggle and decide how great an effort it justifies; indeed, it is generally not difficult to arrive at a compromise which is more advantageous to both contending parties than even a successful battle. But when there is no objective there is no longer any common measure or proportion; no balance or comparison of alternatives is possible, and compromise is inconceivable. In such circumstances the importance of the battle can only be measured by the sacrifices it demands, and from this it follows that the sacrifices already incurred are a perpetual argument for new ones. Thus there would never be any reason to stop killing and dying, except that there is fortunately a limit to human endurance. This paradox is so extreme as to defy analysis. And yet the most perfect example of it is known to every so-called educated man, but, by a sort of taboo, we read it without understanding.

The Greeks and Trojans massacred one another for ten years on account of Helen. Not one of them except the dilettante warrior Paris cared two straws about her; all of them agreed in wishing she had never been born. The person of Helen was so obviously out of scale with this gigantic struggle that in the eyes of all she was no more than the symbol of what was really at stake; but the real issue was never defined by anyone, nor could it be, because it did not exist. For the same reason it could not be calculated. Its importance was simply imagined as corresponding to the deaths incurred and the further massacres expected; and this implied an importance beyond all reckoning. Hector foresaw that his city would be destroyed, his father and brothers massacred, his wife degraded to a slavery worse than death; Achilles knew that he was condemning his father to the miseries and humiliations of a defenceless old age; all were aware that their long absence at the war would bring ruin on their homes; yet no one felt that the cost was too great, because they were all in pursuit of a literal nonentity whose only value was in the price paid for it. When the Greeks began to think of returning to their homes it seemed to Minerva and Ulysses that a reminder of the sufferings of their dead comrades was a sufficient argument to put them to shame. They used, in fact, exactly the same arguments as three thousand years later were employed by Poincaré to castigate the proposal for a negotiated peace. Nowadays the popular mind has an explanation for this sombre zeal in piling up useless ruin; it imagines the machinations of economic interests. But there is no need to look so far. In the time of Homer's Greeks there were no organized bronze manufacturers or international cartels. The truth is that the role which we attribute to mysterious economic oligarchies was attributed by Homer's contemporaries to the gods of the Greek mythology. But there is no need of gods or conspiracies to make men rush headlong into the most absurd disasters. Human nature suffices.

For the clear-sighted, there is no more distressing symptom of this truth than the unreal character of most of the conflicts that are taking place today. They have even less reality than the war between the Greeks and Trojans. At the heart of the Trojan War there was at least a woman and, what is more, a woman of perfect beauty. For our contemporaries the role of Helen is played by words with capital letters. If we grasp one of

3

these words, all swollen with blood and tears, and squeeze it, we find it is empty. Words with content and meaning are not murderous. If one of them occasionally becomes associated with bloodshed, it is rather by chance than by inevitability, and the resulting action is generally controlled and efficacious. But when empty words are given capital letters, then, on the slightest pretext, men will begin shedding blood for them and piling up ruin in their name, without effectively grasping anything to which they refer, since what they refer to can never have any reality, for the simple reason that they mean nothing. In these conditions, the only definition of success is to crush a rival group of men who have a hostile word on their banners; for it is a characteristic of these empty words that each of them has its complementary antagonist. It is true, of course, that not all of these words are intrinsically meaningless; some of them do have meaning if one takes the trouble to define them properly. But when a word is properly defined it loses its capital letter and can no longer serve either as a banner or as a hostile slogan; it becomes simply a sign, helping us to grasp some concrete reality or concrete objective, or method of activity. To clarify thought, to discredit the intrinsically meaningless words, and to define the use of others by precise analysis – to do this, strange though it may appear, might be a way of saving human lives.

Our age seems almost entirely unfitted for such a task. The glossy surface of our civilization hides a real intellectual decadence. There is no area in our minds reserved for superstition, such as the Greeks had in their mythology; and superstition, under cover of an abstract vocabulary, has revenged itself by invading the entire realm of thought. Our science is like a store filled with the most subtle intellectual devices for solving the most complex problems, and yet we are almost incapable of applying the elementary principles of rational thought. In every sphere, we seem to have lost the very elements of intelligence: the ideas of limit, measure, degree, proportion, relation, comparison, contingency, interdependence, interrelation of means and ends. To keep to the social level, our political universe is peopled exclusively by myths and monsters; all it contains is absolutes and abstract entities. This is illustrated by all the words of our political and social vocabulary: nation, security, capitalism, communism, fascism, order, authority, property, democracy. We never use them in phrases such as: There is democracy *to the extent that* . . . or: There is capitalism *in so far as* . . . The use of expressions like 'to the extent that' is beyond our intellectual capacity. Each of these words seems to represent for us an absolute reality, unaffected by conditions, or an absolute objective, independent of methods of action, or an absolute evil; and at the same time we make all these words mean, successively or simultaneously, anything whatsoever. Our lives are lived, in actual fact, among changing, varying realities, subject to the casual play of external necessities, and modifying themselves according to specific conditions within specific limits; and yet we act and strive and sacrifice ourselves and others by reference to fixed and isolated abstractions which cannot possibly be related either to one another or to any concrete facts. In this so-called age of technicians, the only battles we know how to fight are battles against windmills.

So it is easy to find examples of lethal absurdity wherever one looks. The prime specimen is the antagonism between nations. People often try to explain this as a simple cover for capitalist rivalries; but in so doing they ignore a glaringly obvious fact, namely, that the worldwide and complex system of capitalist rivalries and wars and alliances in no way corresponds to the world's division into nations. Two French groups, in the form of limited companies, for example, may find themselves opposed to one another while each of them is in alliance with a German group. The German steel industry may be regarded with hostility by producers of steel goods in France; but it makes little difference to the mining companies whether the iron of Lorraine is worked in France or Germany; and the wine-growers, manufacturers of Parisian articles, and others have an interest in the prosperity of German industry. In the light of these elementary truths the current explanation of international rivalry breaks down. Whoever insists that nationalism is always a cover for capitalist greed should specify whose greed. The mining companies'? The electricity companies'? The steel magnates'? The textile industry's? The banks'? It cannot be all of them, because their interests do not coincide; and if one is referring only to a minority of them, then one must show how it is that this minority has got control of the State. It is true that the policy of a State at any given moment always coincides with the interests of some sector of capitalism, and this offers an explanation whose very superficiality makes it applicable everywhere. But in view of the international circulation of capital it is not clear why a capitalist should look to his own State for protection rather than to some foreign State, or why he should not find it as easy to use pressure and influence with foreign statesmen as with those of his own country. The world's economic structure coincides with its political structure only in so far as States exert their authority in economic affairs; and, moreover, the way they use this authority is not explicable solely in terms of economic interest. If we examine the term 'national interest' we find it does not even mean the interest of capitalist business. 'A man thinks he is dying for his country,' said Anatole France, 'but he is dying for a few industrialists.' But even that is saying too much. What one dies for is not even so substantial and tangible as an industrialist.

The national interest cannot be defined as a common interest of the great industrial, commercial, and financial companies of a country, because there is no such common interest; nor can it be defined as the life, liberty, and well-being of the citizens, because they are continually being adjured to sacrifice their well-being, their liberty, and their lives to the national interest. In the end, a study of modern history leads to the conclusion that the national interest of every State consists in its capacity to make war. In 1911 France nearly went to war for Morocco; but why was Morocco so important? Because the populations of North Africa would make a reserve of cannon fodder; and because, for the purpose of war, a country needs to make its economy as self-supporting as possible in raw materials and markets. What a country calls its vital economic interests are not the things which enable its citizens to live, but the things which enable it to make war; petrol is much more likely than wheat to be a cause of international conflict. Thus when war is waged it is for the purpose of safeguarding or increasing one's capacity to make war. International politics are wholly involved in this vicious circle. What is called national prestige consists in behaving always in such a way as to demoralize other nations by giving them the impression that, if it comes to war, one would certainly defeat them. What is called national security is an imaginary state of affairs in which one would retain the capacity to make war while depriving all other countries of it. It amounts to this, that a self-respecting nation is ready for anything, including war, except for a renunciation of its option to make war. But why is it so essential to be able to make war? No one knows, any more than the Trojans knew why it was necessary for them to keep Helen. That is why the good intentions of peace-loving statesmen are so ineffectual. If the countries were divided by a real opposition of interests, it would be possible to arrive at satisfactory compromises. But when economic and political interests have no meaning apart from war, how can they be peacefully reconciled? It is the very concept of the nation that needs to be suppressed – or rather, the manner in which the word is used. For the word 'national' and the expressions of which it forms part are empty of all meaning; their only content is millions of corpses, and orphans, and disabled men, and tears and despair.

Another good example of murderous absurdity is the opposition between fascism and communism. The fact that this opposition constitutes today a double threat of civil war and world war is perhaps the gravest of all our symptoms of intellectual atrophy, because one has only to examine the present-day meaning of the two words to discover two almost identical political and social conceptions. In each of them the State seizes control of almost every department of individual and social life; in each there is the same frenzied militarization, and the same artificial unanimity, obtained by coercion, in favour of a single party which identifies itself with the State and derives its character from this false identification, and finally there is the same serfdom imposed upon the working masses in place of the ordinary wage system. No two nations are more similar in structure than Germany and Russia, each threatening an international crusade against the other and each pretending to see the other as the Beast of the Apocalypse. Therefore one can safely assert that the opposition between fascism and communism is strictly meaningless. Victory for fascism can only mean extermination of the communists and victory for communism extermination of the fascists. In these circumstances it follows, of course, that anti-fascism and anti-communism are also meaningless. The anti-fascist position is this: anything rather than fascism; anything, including fascism, so long as it is labelled communism. And the anti-communist position: anything rather than communism; anything, including communism, so long as it is labelled fascism. For such a noble cause everyone in either camp is resolved to die, and above all to kill. In Berlin, in the summer of 1932, it was common to see a little group of people gather around two workmen or two petty bourgeois, one a communist and the other a Nazi, who were arguing. After a time it always became clear to both disputants that they were defending exactly the same programme; and this made their heads swim, but it only exacerbated in each of them his hatred for an opponent separated from him by such a gulf as to remain an enemy even when expressing the same ideas. That was four and a half years ago; the Nazis are still torturing German communists in the concentration camps today, and it is possible that France is threatened with a war of extermination between anti-fascists and anti-communists. If such a war took place it would make the Trojan war look perfectly reasonable by comparison; for even if the Greek poet was wrong who said that there was only Helen's phantom at Troy, a phantom Helen is a substantial reality compared to the distinction between fascism and communism.

The distinction between dictatorship and democracy, however, which is related to that between order and freedom, is indeed an example of a real opposition. Nevertheless, it loses its meaning if we see each of the two terms as a thing-in-itself, as is usually done nowadays, instead of seeing it as a point of reference for judging the character of a social structure. It is clear that neither absolute dictatorship nor absolute democracy exists anywhere, and that every social organism everywhere is always a compound of democracy and dictatorship in different proportions; it is clear, too, that the extent to which there is democracy is defined by the relations between different parts of the social mechanism and upon the conditions which control its functioning; it is therefore upon these relations and these conditions that we should try to act. Instead of which we generally imagine that dictatorship or democracy are intrinsically inherent in certain groups of men, whether nations or parties, so that we become obsessed with the desire to crush one or other of these groups, according to whether we are temperamentally more attached to order or to liberty. Many Frenchmen, for example, believe in all good faith that a military victory for France over Germany would be a victory for democracy. As they see it, freedom inheres in the French nation and tyranny in the German, in much the same way that for Molière's contemporaries there was a dormitive virtue inherent in opium. If a day comes when the requirements of so-called 'national defence' transform France into a fortified camp in which the whole nation is totally subjected to the military authority, and if this transformed France goes to war with Germany, then these Frenchmen will allow themselves to be killed, having first killed as many Germans as possible, in the touching belief that their blood is being shed for democracy. It does not occur to them that dictatorship arose in Germany as the result of certain conditions and that an alteration of those conditions, in such a way as to make possible some relaxation of the State authority in Germany, might be more effective than killing the young men of Berlin and Hamburg.

Another example: suppose one dared to suggest to any party man the idea of an armistice in Spain. If he is a man of the right he will indignantly reply that the fight must continue until the forces of order are triumphant and anarchy is crushed; if he is a man of the left he will reply with equal indignation that the fight must continue until the people's freedom and well-being are assured and the oppressors and exploiters crushed. The man of the right forgets that no political regime, of whatever kind, involves disorders remotely comparable to those of a civil war, with its deliberate destruction, its non-stop massacre in the firing line, its slowing down of production, and the hundreds of crimes it permits every day, on both sides, by the fact that any hooligan can get hold of a gun. The man of the left, for his part, forgets that even on his own side liberty is suppressed far more drastically by the necessities of civil war than it would be by the coming to power of a party of the extreme right; in other words, he forgets that there is a state of siege, that militarization is in force both at the front and behind it, that there is a police terror, and that the individual has no security and no protection against arbitrary injustice; he forgets, too, that the cost of the war, and the ruin it causes, and the slowing down of production condemn the people to a long period of far more cruel privation than their exploiters would. And both of them forget that during the long months of civil war an almost identical regime has grown up on both sides. Each of them has unconsciously lost sight of his ideal and replaced it by an entity without substance. For each, the victory of what he still calls his idea can no longer mean anything except the extermination of the enemy; and each of them will scorn any suggestion of peace, replying to it with the same knockout argument as Minerva in Homer and Poincaré in 1917: 'The dead do not wish it.'

Of all the conflicts which set groups of men against one another the most legitimate and serious – one could perhaps say, the only serious one – is what is called today the *class struggle* (an expression which needs clarifying). But this is only true in so far as it is not confused by imaginary entities which obstruct controlled action, lead efforts astray, and entail the risk of ineradicable hatred, idiotic destructiveness, and senseless butchery. What is well founded, vital, and essential is the eternal struggle of those who obey against those who command when the mechanism of social power involves a disregard for the human dignity of the former. It is an eternal struggle because those who command are always inclined, whether they know it or not, to trample on the human dignity of those below them. The function of command cannot, except in special cases, be exercised in a way that respects the personal humanity of those who carry out orders. When exercised as though men were objects, and unresisting ones at that, it inevitably acts upon them as exceptionally pliable objects; for a man exposed to the threat of death, which is really the final sanction of all authority, can become more pliable than inert matter. So long as there is a stable social hierarchy, of whatever form, those at the bottom must struggle so as not to lose all the rights of a human being. But the resistance of those at the top, although it usually appears unjust, is also inspired by concrete motives. First, personal motives; for except in rather rare cases of generosity the privileged hate to lose any of their material and moral privileges. But there are also higher motives. To those in whom the functions of command are vested it seems to be their duty to defend order, without which no social life can survive; and the only order they conceive is the existing one. Nor are they entirely wrong, for until a different order has been, in fact, established no one can say with certainty that it is possible. It is just for this reason that social progress depends upon a pressure from below sufficient to change effectively the relations of power and thus to compel the actual establishment of new social relationships. The tension between pressure from below and resistance from above creates and maintains an unstable equilibrium, which defines at each moment the structure of a society. This tension is a struggle but not a war;

and although it may in certain circumstances turn into a war, it does not inevitably do so. The story of the interminable and useless massacres around Troy is not our only legacy from antiquity; there is also the vigorous and concerted action of the Roman plebeians, who, without shedding a drop of blood, escaped from a condition verging upon slavery and obtained the institution of tribunes to guarantee their new rights. In exactly the same way the French workers, by occupying the factories, without violence, enforced the recognition of certain elementary rights and obtained elected delegates to guarantee them.

But early Rome had one important advantage over modern France. In social matters she knew nothing of abstract entities, or words in capitals, or words ending in -ism; nor any of those things which, with us, are liable to stultify the most serious efforts or to degrade the social struggle into a war as ruinous, as bloody, and as irrational in every way as a war between nations. On inspection, almost all the words and phrases of our political vocabulary turn out to be hollow. What, for example, can be the meaning of that slogan which was so popular at the recent elections – 'the fight against the trusts'? A trust is an economic monopoly in the hands of financial powers, which is used by them not in the public interest but in such a way as to increase their own influence. What is it that is wrong about this? The fact that a monopoly is serving as the instrument of a will-to-power uninterested in the public good. But it is not this fact that is attacked; what is attacked is the fact, which is in itself morally indifferent, that the will-to-power belongs to an economic oligarchy. The aim is to replace economic oligarchies by the State, which has a will-to-power of its own and is quite as little concerned with the public good; and a will-to-power, moreover, which is not economic but military and therefore much more dangerous to any good folk who have a taste for staying alive. And on the bourgeois side what on earth is the sense of objecting to State control in economic affairs if one accepts private monopolies which have all the economic and technical disadvantages of State monopolies and possibly some others as well? One could make a long list of pairs of complementary slogans of this kind, all of them equally unreal. The two considered above are relatively harmless, but this is not true of all of them.

For example, whatever can be in the heads of those for whom the word 'capitalism' signifies the absolute of evil? The society in which we live includes forms of coercion and oppression by which those who suffer from them are all too often overwhelmed; it includes the most grievous inequalities and unnecessary miseries. On the other hand, the economic character of this society consists in certain methods of production, consumption, and exchange, which are continually varying, however, and which depend upon certain fundamental relationships: between the production and the circulation of goods, between the circulation of goods and money, between money and production, between money and consumption. This whole interplay of varied and changing economic phenomena is arbitrarily converted into an abstraction, which defies all definition, and is then made responsible, under the name of capitalism, for every hardship endured by oneself or others. After that, it is only natural that any man of character should devote his life to the destruction of capitalism, or rather (it comes to the same thing) to revolution – for this negative meaning is the only one possessed today by the word revolution.

Since the 'destruction of capitalism' has no meaning – capitalism being an abstraction – and since it does not refer to any precise modifications that might be applied to the regime (such modifications are contemptuously dismissed as 'reforms'), the slogan can only imply the destruction of capitalists and, more generally, of everyone who does not call himself an opponent of capitalism. Apparently it is easier to kill, and even to die, than to ask ourselves a few quite simple questions like the following: Can the laws and conventions which control our present economic life be said to constitute a system? To what extent is this or that feature of our economic life necessarily connected with the others? To what extent would the modification of this or that economic law produce repercussions among the others? How far can the ills arising from the social relations which exist today be attributed to this or that convention and how far are they attributable to the totality of conventions of our economic life? How far are they attributable to other factors, either permanent factors which would persist after the transformation of the economic system or, on the contrary, factors which could be eliminated without putting an end to what is called the regime? What kind of hardships, either transitory or permanent, would necessarily be involved by the chosen method for transforming the regime? What new hardships might be introduced by the proposed new organization of society? If we gave serious thought to these problems we might reach the point where we could give some meaning to the assertion that capitalism is an evil; but we should mean only a relative evil, and the proposal to transform the regime would be only for the purpose of substituting a lesser evil. And the proposed transformation would be a clearly defined and limited one.

The same criticism is applicable in its entirety to those in the opposite camp, except that the concern for maintaining order replaces the concern about the sufferings of the depressed social classes and the instinct of conservation replaces the desire for change. The bourgeois always tend to regard anyone who wishes to put an end to capitalism, and sometimes even anyone who wants to reform it, as an agent of disorder; and they do so because they are ignorant as to what extent and in what circumstances the various economic relations, which are subsumed today under the general name of capitalism, are factors in preserving order. Many of them are in favour of changing nothing, because they do not know what modifications of the system may or may not be dangerous; they fail to realize that, since conditions are always changing, the refusal to modify the system is itself a modification which may be productive of disorders. Most of them appeal to economic laws as religiously as if they were the unwritten laws invoked by Antigone, and this although they can see them changing day by day in front of their eyes. The preservation of the capitalist regime is a meaningless expression, in their mouths, because they do not know what ought to be preserved, nor how much of it; all they can mean, in practice, is the suppression of everyone who wants to put an end to the regime. The struggle between the opponents and the defenders of capitalism is a struggle between innovators who do not know what innovation to make and conservatives who do not know what to conserve; it is a battle of blind men struggling in a void, and for that very reason it is liable to become a war of extermination. The same situation exists on a smaller scale in the struggle within any industrial firm. In general, the worker instinctively blames his employer for all the hardships of work in a factory; he does not ask himself whether under any other property system the management would not inflict some of the same hardships on him, or indeed exactly the same ones, or even perhaps some worse ones; nor does he ask himself how many of these hardships might be abolished, by abolishing their causes, without any alteration of the existing property system. He identifies the struggle 'against the boss' with the undying protest of the human being oppressed by too many hardships. The head of the firm, for his part, is rightly concerned to maintain his authority. But his authority is strictly limited to overall direction, to the due coordination of the branches of production, and to ensuring, with some compulsion if necessary, that the work is properly executed. Any industrial regime, of whatever kind, in which these functions of coordination and control can be effectively exercised is allowing sufficient authority to the heads of the firms. But the feeling of authority, in these men's minds, is especially connected with a certain atmosphere of deference and subservience which has no necessary connection with a high standard of work; and, above all, when they become aware of latent or overt opposition among their personnel they always attribute it to certain individuals, whereas in reality a spirit of revolt, whether loud or silent, aggressive or despairing, is always present wherever life is physically or morally oppressive. In the worker's mind the struggle 'against the boss' is confused with the assertion of human dignity, and in the manager's mind the struggle against the 'ringleaders' is confused with his duty to the job and his professional conscience. Both of them are tilting at windmills, so their efforts cannot be confined to reasonable objectives. When strikes are undertaken for clearly defined claims a settlement is attainable without too great difficulty, as we have sometimes seen; but we have also seen strikes which resembled wars, in the sense that neither side had any objective, strikes in which there were no real or tangible issues – apart from arrested production, deteriorating machines, destitution, want, weeping women, and hungry children; and such bitterness on both sides that any agreement seemed impossible. In events like these there are the seeds of civil war.

If we analysed in this way all the words and formulas which have served throughout history to call forth the spirit of self-sacrifice and cruelty combined, we should doubtless discover them all to be just as empty. And yet, all these bloodthirsty abstractions must have some sort of connection with real life; and indeed they have. It may be that there was only Helen's phantom at Troy, but the Greek and Trojan armies were not phantoms; and in the same way although there is no meaning in the word 'nation' and the slogans in which it occurs, the different States with their offices, prisons, arsenals, barracks, and customs are real enough. The theoretical distinction between the two forms of totalitarian regime, fascism and communism, is imaginary, but in Germany in 1932 there existed very concretely two political organizations each of which wanted to achieve complete power and consequently to exterminate the other. A democratic party may gradually change into a party of dictatorship but it still remains distinct from the dictatorial party it is striving to suppress. France, for the purpose of defence against Germany, may submit in her turn to a totalitarian regime, but the French State and the German State will not cease to be two separate States. Both the destruction and the preservation of capitalism are meaningless slogans, but these slogans are supported by real organizations. Corresponding to each empty abstraction there is an actual human group, and any abstraction of which this is not true remains harmless. Conversely, any group which has not secreted an abstract entity will probably not be dangerous. This particular kind of secretion is superbly illustrated by the 'Dr Knock' of Jules Romains with his maxim: 'Above the interest of the patient and the interest of the doctor stands the interest of Medicine.' It is pure comedy, because the medical profession has not so far secreted such an entity; it is always by organizations concerned with guarding or acquiring power that these entities are secreted. All the absurdities which make history look like a prolonged delirium have their root in one essential absurdity, which is the nature of power. The necessity for power is obvious, because life cannot be lived without order; but the allocation of power is arbitrary because all men are alike, or very nearly. Yet power must not seem to be arbitrarily allocated, because it will not then be recognized as power. Therefore prestige, which is illusion, is of the very essence of power. All power is based, in fact, upon the interrelation of human activities; but in order to be stable it must appear as something absolute and sacrosanct, both to those who wield and those who submit to it and also to other external powers. The conditions which ensure order are essentially contradictory, and men seem to be compelled to choose between the anarchy which goes with inadequate power and the wars of every kind which go with the preoccupation of prestige.

All the absurdities we have enumerated cease to appear absurd when translated into the language of power. Is it not natural that every State should define the national interest as the capacity to make war, when it is surrounded by States capable of subduing it by arms if it is weak? One must either join the race to prepare for war or else be resigned to enduring whatever some other armed State may choose to inflict; no third choice seems possible. Nothing but complete and universal disarmament could resolve this dilemma, and that is hardly conceivable. And, further, a State cannot appear weak in its external relations without the risk of weakening its authority with its own subjects. If Priam and Hector had delivered Helen to the Greeks this might merely have increased the Greeks' inclination to sack a town that seemed so ill prepared to defend itself; and they would also have risked a general uprising in Troy – not because the Trojans would have been upset by the surrender of Helen, but because it would have suggested to them that their chiefs could not be so very powerful. In Spain, if one of the two sides gave the impression of wanting peace this would first have the effect of encouraging its enemies and stimulating their aggressiveness, and then it would involve the risk of uprisings among its own supporters. Again, for a man who is outside both the anti-communist and the anti-fascist blocs the clash between two almost identical ideologies may appear ridiculous; but since these two blocs exist the members of one of them are bound to see absolute evil in the other, because it will exterminate them if they are

the weaker. The leaders on each side must seem prepared to annihilate the enemy, in order to maintain
their authority with their own troops; and once these
blocs have achieved a certain degree of power, neutral-
ity becomes an almost untenable position. In the same
way, when those at the bottom of any social hierarchy
begin to fear that unless they dispossess those above
them they will be completely crushed, then, so soon as
either side becomes strong enough to have nothing to
fear, it will yield to the intoxication of power mixed with
spite. Power, in general, is always essentially vulnerable;
and therefore it is bound to defend itself, for otherwise
society would lack the necessary minimum of stability.
But it is nearly always believed, with or without reason,
by all parties, that the only defence is attack. And it is
natural that the most implacable conflicts should arise
out of imaginary disputes, because these take place
solely on the level of power and prestige. It would probably be easier for France to cede raw materials to
Germany than a few acres of ground with the title of
'colony', and easier for Germany to do without raw
materials than without the title of 'colonial power'. The
essential contradiction in human society is that every
social status quo rests upon an equilibrium of forces or
pressures, similar to the equilibrium of fluids; but
between one prestige and another there can be no equilibrium. Prestige has no bounds and its satisfaction
always involves the infringement of someone else's
prestige or dignity. And prestige is inseparable from
power. This seems to be an impasse from which

humanity can only escape by some miracle. But human life is made up of miracles. Who would believe that a Gothic cathedral could remain standing if we did not see it every day? Since the state of war is not, in fact, continuous, it is not impossible that peace might continue indefinitely. Once all the real data of a problem have been revealed the problem is well on the way to solution. The problem of peace, both international and social, has never yet been completely stated.

What prevents us from seeing the data of the problem is the swarm of vacuous entities or abstractions; they even prevent us from seeing that there is a problem to be solved, instead of a fatality to be endured. They stupefy the mind; they not only make men willing to die but, infinitely worse, they make them forget the value of life. To sweep away these entities from every department of political and social life is an urgently necessary measure of public hygiene. But the operation is not an easy one; the whole intellectual climate of our age favours the growth and multiplication of vacuous entities. Perhaps we should begin with a reform of our methods of scientific education and popularization, abolishing the artificial vocabulary which those methods crudely and superstitiously encourage. By reviving the intelligent use of expressions like *to the extent that, in so far as, on condition that, in relation to,* and by discrediting all those vicious arguments which amount to proclaiming the dormitive virtue of opium, we might be rendering a highly important practical service to our contemporaries. A general raising of the intellectual level would greatly assist any educational attempt to deflate the imaginary causes of strife. As things are, there is certainly no shortage of preachers of appeasement in every sphere; but their sermons, as a rule, are not intended to awaken intelligence and eliminate unreal conflicts, but rather, by inducing somnolence, to obscure real conflicts. There are no more dangerous enemies of international and social peace than those spellbinders whose talk about peace between nations means simply an indefinite prolongation of the status quo for the exclusive advantage of the French State or those whose advocacy of social peace presupposes the safeguarding of privilege, or at least the right of the privileged to veto any change they dislike. The relations between social forces are essentially variable, and the underprivileged will always seek to alter them; it is wrong to enforce an artificial stabilization. What is required is discrimination between the imaginary and the real, so as to diminish the risks of war, without interfering with the struggle between forces which, according to Heraclitus, is the condition of life itself.

Human Personality

'You do not interest me.' No man can say these words to another without committing a cruelty and offending against justice.

'Your person does not interest me.' These words can be used in an affectionate conversation between close friends, without jarring upon even the tenderest nerve of their friendship.

In the same way, one can say without degrading oneself, 'My person does not count', but not 'I do not count'.

This proves that something is amiss with the vocabulary of the modern trend of thought known as Personalism. And in this domain, where there is a grave error of vocabulary it is almost certainly the sign of a grave error of thought.

There is something sacred in every man, but it is not his person. Nor yet is it the human personality. It is this man; no more and no less.

I see a passer-by in the street. He has long arms, blue eyes, and a mind whose thoughts I do not know, but perhaps they are commonplace.

It is neither his person nor the human personality in him which is sacred to me. It is he. The whole of him.

The arms, the eyes, the thoughts, everything. Not without infinite scruple would I touch anything of this.

If it were the human personality in him that was sacred to me, I could easily put out his eyes. As a blind man he would be exactly as much a human personality as before. I should not have touched the person in him at all. I should have destroyed nothing but his eyes.

It is impossible to define what is meant by respect for human personality. It is not just that it cannot be defined in words. That can be said of many perfectly clear ideas. But this one cannot be conceived either; it cannot be defined nor isolated by the silent operation of the mind.

To set up as a standard of public morality a notion which can be neither defined nor conceived is to open the door to every kind of tyranny.

The notion of rights, which was launched into the world in 1789, has proved unable, because of its intrinsic inadequacy, to fulfil the role assigned to it.

To combine two inadequate notions, by talking about the rights of human personality, will not bring us any further.

What is it, exactly, that prevents me from putting that man's eyes out if I am allowed to do so and if it takes my fancy?

Although it is the whole of him that is sacred to me, he is not sacred in all respects and from every point of view. He is not sacred in as much as he happens to have long arms, blue eyes, or possibly commonplace thoughts. Nor as a duke, if he is one; nor as a dustman, if that is what he is. Nothing of all this would stay my hand.

What would stay it is the knowledge that if someone were to put out his eyes, his soul would be lacerated by the thought that harm was being done to him.

At the bottom of the heart of every human being, from earliest infancy until the tomb, there is something that goes on indomitably expecting, in the teeth of all experience of crimes committed, suffered, and witnessed, that good and not evil will be done to him. It is this above all that is sacred in every human being.

The good is the only source of the sacred. There is nothing sacred except the good and what pertains to it.

This profound and childlike and unchanging expectation of good in the heart is not what is involved when we agitate for our rights. The motive which prompts a little boy to watch jealously to see if his brother has a slightly larger piece of cake arises from a much more superficial level of the soul. The word justice means two very different things according to whether it refers to the one or the other level. It is only the former one that matters.

Every time that there arises from the depths of a human heart the childish cry which Christ himself could not restrain, 'Why am I being hurt?', then there is certainly injustice. For if, as often happens, it is only the result of a misunderstanding, then the injustice consists in the inadequacy of the explanation.

Those people who inflict the blows which provoke this cry are prompted by different motives according to temperament or occasion. There are some people who get a positive pleasure from the cry; and many others simply do not hear it. For it is a silent cry, which sounds only in the secret heart.

These two states of mind are closer than they appear to be. The second is only a weaker mode of the first; its deafness is complacently cultivated because it is agreeable and it offers a positive satisfaction of its own. There are no other restraints upon our will than material necessity and the existence of other human beings around us. Any imaginary extension of these limits is seductive, so there is a seduction in whatever helps us to forget the reality of the obstacles. That is why upheavals like war and civil war are so intoxicating; they empty human lives of their reality and seem to turn people into puppets. That is also why slavery is so pleasant to the masters.

In those who have suffered too many blows, in slaves for example, that place in the heart from which the infliction of evil evokes a cry of surprise may seem to be dead. But it is never quite dead; it is simply unable to cry out any more. It has sunk into a state of dumb and ceaseless lamentation.

And even in those who still have the power to cry out, the cry hardly ever expresses itself, either, inwardly or outwardly, in coherent language. Usually, the words through which it seeks expression are quite irrelevant.

That is all the more inevitable because those who most often have occasion to feel that evil is being done to them are those who are least trained in the art of speech. Nothing, for example, is more frightful than to see some poor wretch in the police court stammering before a magistrate who keeps up an elegant flow of witticisms.

Apart from the intelligence, the only human faculty which has an interest in public freedom of expression is that point in the heart which cries out against evil. But as it cannot express itself, freedom is of little use to it. What is first needed is a system of public education capable of providing it, so far as possible, with means of expression; and next, a regime in which the public freedom of expression is characterized not so much by freedom as by an attentive silence in which this faint and inept cry can make itself heard; and finally, institutions are needed of a sort which will, so far as possible, put power into the hands of men who are able and anxious to hear and understand it.

Clearly, a political party busily seeking, or maintaining itself in power can discern nothing in these cries except a noise. Its reaction will be different according to whether the noise interferes with or contributes to that of its own propaganda. But it can never be capable of the tender and sensitive attention which is needed to understand its meaning.

The same is true to a lesser degree of organizations contaminated by party influences; in other words, when public life is dominated by a party system, it is true of all organizations, including, for example, trade unions and even churches.

Naturally, too, parties and similar organizations are equally insensitive to intellectual scruples.

So when freedom of expression means in fact no

more than freedom of propaganda for organizations of this kind, there is in fact no free expression for the only parts of the human soul that deserve it. Or if there is any, it is infinitesimal; hardly more than in a totalitarian system.

And this is how it is in a democracy where the party system controls the distribution of power; which is what we call democracy in France, for up to now we have known no other. We must therefore invent something different.

Applying the same criterion in the same way to any public institution we can reach equally obvious conclusions.

It is not the person which provides this criterion. When the infliction of evil provokes a cry of sorrowful surprise from the depth of the soul, it is not a personal thing. Injury to the personality and its desires is not sufficient to evoke it, but only and always the sense of contact with injustice through pain. It is always, in the last of men as in Christ himself, an impersonal protest.

There are also many cries of personal protest, but they are unimportant; you may provoke as many of them as you wish without violating anything sacred.

So far from its being his person, what is sacred in a human being is the impersonal in him.

Everything which is impersonal in man is sacred, and nothing else.

In our days, when writers and scientists have so oddly

usurped the place of priests, the public acknowledges, with a totally unjustified docility, that the artistic and scientific faculties are sacred. This is generally held to be self-evident, though it is very far from being so. If any reason is felt to be called for, people allege that the free play of these faculties is one of the highest manifestations of the human personality.

Often it is, indeed, no more than that. In which case it is easy to see how much it is worth and what can be expected from it.

One of its results is the sort of attitude which is summed up in Blake's horrible saying: 'Sooner murder an infant in its cradle than nurse unacted desires', or the attitude which breeds the idea of the 'gratuitous act'. Another result is a science in which every possible standard, criterion, and value is recognized except truth.

Gregorian chant, Romanesque architecture, the *Iliad,* the invention of geometry were not, for the people through whom they were brought into being and made available to us, occasions for the manifestation of personality.

When science, art, literature, and philosophy are simply the manifestation of personality they are on a level where glorious and dazzling achievements are possible, which can make a man's name live for thousands of years. But above this level, far above, separated by an abyss, is the level where the highest things are achieved. These things are essentially anonymous.

It is pure chance whether the names of those who

reach this level are preserved or lost; even when they are remembered they have become anonymous. Their personality has vanished.

Truth and beauty dwell on this level of the impersonal and the anonymous. This is the realm of the sacred; on the other level nothing is sacred, except in the sense that we might say this of a touch of colour in a picture if it represented the Eucharist.

What is sacred in science is truth; what is sacred in art is beauty. Truth and beauty are impersonal. All this is too obvious.

If a child is doing a sum and does it wrong, the mistake bears the stamp of his personality. If he does the sum exactly right, his personality does not enter into it at all.

Perfection is impersonal. Our personality is the part of us which belongs to error and sin. The whole effort of the mystic has always been to become such that there is no part left in his soul to say 'I'.

But the part of the soul which says 'We' is infinitely more dangerous still.

Impersonality is only reached by the practice of a form of attention which is rare in itself and impossible except in solitude; and not only physical but mental solitude. This is never achieved by a man who thinks of himself as a member of a collectivity, as part of something which says 'We'.

Men as parts of a collectivity are debarred from even the lower forms of the impersonal. A group of human beings cannot even add two and two. Working out a sum takes place in a mind temporarily oblivious of the existence of any other minds.

Although the personal and the impersonal are opposed, there is a way from the one to the other. But there is no way from the collective to the impersonal. A collectivity must dissolve into separate persons before the impersonal can be reached.

This is the only sense in which the person has more of the sacred than the collectivity.

The collectivity is not only alien to the sacred, but it deludes us with a false imitation of it.

Idolatry is the name of the error which attributes a sacred character to the collectivity; and it is the commonest of crimes, at all times, at all places. The man for whom the development of personality is all that counts has totally lost all sense of the sacred; and it is hard to know which of these errors is the worst. They are often found combined, in various proportions, in the same mind. But the second error is much less powerful and enduring than the first.

Spiritually, the struggle between Germany and France in 1940 was in the main not a struggle between barbarism and civilization or between evil and good, but between the first of these two errors and the second. The victory of the former is not surprising; it is by nature the stronger.

There is nothing scandalous in the subordination of the person to the collectivity; it is a mechanical fact of the same order as the inferiority of a gram to a kilogram on the scales. The person is in fact always subordinate to the collectivity, even in its so-called free expression.

For example, it is precisely those artists and writers who are most inclined to think of their art as the manifestation of their personality who are in fact the most in bondage to public taste. Hugo had no difficulty in reconciling the cult of the self with his role of 'resounding echo'; and examples like Wilde, Gide, and the Surrealists are even more obvious. Scientists of the same class are equally enslaved by fashion, which rules over science even more despotically than over the shape of hats. For these men the collective opinion of specialists is practically a dictatorship.

The person, being subordinate to the collective both in fact and by the nature of things, enjoys no natural rights which can be appealed to on its behalf.

It is said, quite correctly, that in antiquity there existed no notion of respect for the person. The ancients thought far too clearly to entertain such a confused idea.

The human being can only escape from the collective by raising himself above the personal and entering into the impersonal. The moment he does this, there is something in him, a small portion of his soul, upon which nothing of the collective can get a hold. If he can root himself in the impersonal good so as to be able to draw energy from it, then he is in a condition, whenever he feels the obligation to do so, to bring to bear without any outside help, against any collectivity, a small but real force.

There are occasions when an almost infinitesimal force can be decisive. A collectivity is much stronger than a single man; but every collectivity depends for its existence upon operations, of which simple addition is the elementary example, which can only be performed by a mind in a state of solitude.

This dependence suggests a method of giving the impersonal a hold on the collective, if only we could find out how to use it.

Every man who has once touched the level of the impersonal is charged with a responsibility towards all human beings; to safeguard, not their persons, but whatever frail potentialities are hidden within them for passing over to the impersonal.

It is primarily to these men that the appeal to respect the sacredness of the human being should be addressed. For such an appeal can have no reality unless it is addressed to someone capable of understanding it.

It is useless to explain to a collectivity that there is something in each of the units composing it which it ought not to violate. To begin with, a collectivity is not someone, except by a fiction; it has only an abstract existence and can only be spoken to fictitiously. And, moreover, if it were someone it would be someone who was not disposed to respect anything except himself.

Further, the chief danger does not lie in the collectivity's tendency to circumscribe the person, but in the person's tendency to immolate himself in the collective. Or perhaps the first danger is only a superficial and deceptive aspect of the second.

Just as it is useless to tell the collectivity that the person is sacred, it is also useless to tell the person so. The person cannot believe it. It does not feel sacred. The reason that prevents the person from feeling sacred is that actually it is not.

If there are some people who feel differently, who feel something sacred in their own persons and believe they can generalize and attribute it to every person, they are under a double illusion.

What they feel is not the authentic sense of the sacred but its false imitation engendered by the collective; and if they feel it in respect of their own person it is because it participates in collective prestige through the social consideration bestowed upon it.

So they are mistaken in thinking they can generalize from their own case. Their motive is generous, but it cannot have enough force to make them really see the mass of people as anything but mere anonymous human matter. But it is hard for them to find this out, because they have no contact with the mass of people.

The person in man is a thing in distress; it feels cold and is always looking for a warm shelter.

But those in whom it is, in fact or in expectation, warmly wrapped in social consideration are unaware of this.

That is why it was not in popular circles that the philosophy of personalism originated and developed, but among writers, for whom it is part of their profession to have or hope to acquire a name and a reputation.

Relations between the collectivity and the person

should be arranged with the sole purpose of removing whatever is detrimental to the growth and mysterious germination of the impersonal element in the soul.

This means, on the one hand, that for every person there should be enough room, enough freedom to plan the use of one's time, the opportunity to reach ever higher levels of attention, some solitude, some silence. At the same time the person needs warmth, lest it be driven by distress to submerge itself in the collective.

If this is the good, then modern societies, even democratic ones, seem to go about as far as it is possible to go in the direction of evil. In particular, a modern factory reaches perhaps almost the limit of horror. Everybody in it is constantly harassed and kept on edge by the interference of extraneous wills while the soul is left in cold and desolate misery. What man needs is silence and warmth; what he is given is an icy pandemonium.

Physical labour may be painful, but it is not degrading as such. It is not art; it is not science; it is something else, possessing an exactly equal value with art and science, for it provides an equal opportunity to reach the impersonal stage of attention.

To take a youth who has a vocation for this kind of work and employ him at a conveyor belt or as a piece-work machinist is no less a crime than to put out the eyes of the young Watteau and make him turn a grindstone. But the painter's vocation can be discerned and the other cannot.

Exactly to the same extent as art and science, though

in a different way, physical labour is a certain contact with the reality, the truth, and the beauty of this universe and with the eternal wisdom which is the order in it.

For this reason it is sacrilege to degrade labour in exactly the same sense that it is sacrilege to trample upon the Eucharist.

If the workers felt this, if they felt that by being the victim they are in a certain sense the accomplice of sacrilege, their resistance would have a very different force from what is provided by the consideration of personal rights. It would not be an economic demand but an impulse from the depth of their being, fierce and desperate like that of a young girl who is being forced into a brothel; and at the same time it would be a cry of hope from the depth of their heart.

This feeling, which surely enough exists in them, is so inarticulate as to be indiscernible even to themselves; and it is not the professionals of speech who can express it for them.

Usually, when addressing them on their conditions, the selected topic is wages; and for men burdened with a fatigue that makes any effort of attention painful it is a relief to contemplate the unproblematic clarity of figures.

In this way, they forget that the subject of the bargain, which they complain they are being forced to sell cheap and for less than the just price, is nothing other than their soul.

Suppose the devil were bargaining for the soul of

some poor wretch and someone, moved by pity, should step in and say to the devil: 'It is a shame for you to bid so low; the commodity is worth at least twice as much.'

Such is the sinister farce which has been played by the working-class movement, its trade unions, its political parties, its leftist intellectuals.

This bargaining spirit was already implicit in the notion of rights which the men of 1789 so unwisely made the keynote of their deliberate challenge to the world. By so doing, they ensured its inefficacy in advance.

The notion of rights is linked with the notion of sharing out, of exchange, of measured quantity. It has a commercial flavour, essentially evocative of legal claims and arguments. Rights are always asserted in a tone of contention; and when this tone is adopted, it must rely upon force in the background, or else it will be laughed at.

There is a number of other notions, all in the same category, which are themselves entirely alien to the supernatural but nevertheless a little superior to brute force. All of them relate to the behaviour of the collective animal, to use Plato's language, while it still exhibits a few traces of the training imposed on it by the supernatural working of grace. If they are not continually revived by a renewal of this working, if they are merely survivals of it, they become necessarily subject to the animal's caprice.

To this category belong the notion of rights, and of personality, and of democracy. As Bernanos had the courage to point out, democracy offers no defence against dictatorship. By the nature of things, the person is subdued to the collectivity, and rights are dependent upon force. The lies and misconceptions which obscure this truth are extremely dangerous because they prevent us from appealing to the only thing which is immune to force and can preserve us from it: namely, that other force which is the radiance of the spirit. It is only in plants, by virtue of the sun's energy caught up by the green leaves and operating in the sap, that inert matter can find its way upward against the law of gravity. A plant deprived of light is gradually but inexorably overcome by gravity and death.

Among the lies in question is the eighteenth-century materialists' notion of natural right. We do not owe this to Rousseau, whose lucid and powerful spirit was of genuinely Christian inspiration, but to Diderot and the Encyclopédistes.

It was from Rome that we inherited the notion of rights, and like everything else that comes from ancient Rome, who is the woman full of the names of blasphemy in the Apocalypse, it is pagan and unbaptizable. The Romans, like Hitler, understood that power is not fully efficacious unless clothed in a few ideas, and to this end they made use of the idea of rights, which is admirably suited to it. Modern Germany has been accused of flouting the idea; but she invoked it *ad nauseam* in her role of deprived, proletarian nation. It is true, of course, that she allows only one right to her victims: obedience. Ancient Rome did the same.

It is singularly monstrous that ancient Rome should be praised for having bequeathed to us the notion of rights. If we examine Roman law in its cradle, to see what species it belongs to, we discover that property was defined by the *jus utendi et abutendi*. And in fact the things which the property owner had the right to use or abuse at will were for the most part human beings.

The Greeks had no conception of rights. They had no words to express it. They were content with the name of justice.

It is extraordinary that Antigone's unwritten law should have been confused with the idea of natural right. In Creon's eyes there was absolutely nothing that was natural in Antigone's behaviour. He thought she was mad.

And we should be the last people to disagree with him; we who at this moment are thinking, talking, and behaving exactly as he did. One has only to consult the text.

Antigone says to Creon: 'It was not Zeus who published that edict; it was not Justice, companion of the gods in the other world, who set such laws among men.' Creon tries to convince her that his orders were just; he accuses her of having outraged one of her brothers by honouring the other, so that the same honour has been paid to the impious and the loyal, to the one who died in the attempt to destroy his own country and the one who died defending it.

She answers: 'Nevertheless the other world demands

43

equal laws.' To which he sensibly objects: 'There can be no equal sharing between a brave man and a traitor', and she has only the absurd reply: 'Who knows whether this holds in the other world?'

Creon's comment is perfectly reasonable: 'A foe is never a friend, not even in death.' And the little simpleton can only reply: 'I was born to share, not hate, but love.'

To which Creon, ever more reasonable: 'Pass, then, to the other world, and if thou must love, love those who dwell there.'

And, truly, this was the right place for her. For the unwritten law which this little girl obeyed had nothing whatsoever in common with rights, or with the natural; it was the same love, extreme and absurd, which led Christ to the Cross.

It was Justice, companion of the gods in the other world, who dictated this surfeit of love, and not any right at all. Rights have no direct connection with love.

Just as the notion of rights is alien to the Greek mind, so also it is alien to the Christian inspiration whenever it is pure and uncontaminated by the Roman, Hebraic, or Aristotelian heritage. One cannot imagine St Francis of Assisi talking about rights.

If you say to someone who has ears to hear: 'What you are doing to me is not just', you may touch and awaken at its source the spirit of attention and love. But it is not the same with words like 'I have the right . . .' or 'you have no right to . . .' They evoke a latent war and awaken the spirit of contention. To place the notion of rights at the centre of social conflicts is to inhibit any possible impulse of charity on both sides.

Relying almost exclusively on this notion, it becomes impossible to keep one's eyes on the real problem. If someone tries to browbeat a farmer to sell his eggs at a moderate price, the farmer can say: 'I have the right to keep my eggs if I don't get a good enough price.' But if a young girl is being forced into a brothel she will not talk about her rights. In such a situation the word would sound ludicrously inadequate.

Thus it is that the social drama, which corresponds to the latter situation, is falsely assimilated, by the use of the word 'rights', to the former one.

Thanks to this word, what should have been a cry of protest from the depth of the heart has been turned into a shrill nagging of claims and counter-claims, which is both impure and unpractical.

The notion of rights, by its very mediocrity, leads on naturally to that of the person, for rights are related to personal things. They are on that level.

It is much worse still if the word 'personal' is added to the word 'rights', thus implying the rights of the personality to what is called full expression. In that case the tone that colours the cry of the oppressed would be even meaner than bargaining. It would be the tone of envy.

For the full expression of personality depends upon its being inflated by social prestige; it is a social privilege. No one mentions this to the masses when haranguing them about personal rights. They are told the opposite; and their minds have not enough analytic power to perceive this truth clearly for themselves. But they feel it; their everyday experience makes them certain of it.

However, this is not a reason for them to reject the slogan. To the dimmed understanding of our age there seems nothing odd in claiming an equal share of privilege for everybody – an equal share in things whose essence is privilege. The claim is both absurd and base; absurd because privilege is, by definition, inequality; and base because it is not worth claiming.

But the category of men who formulate claims, and everything else, the men who have the monopoly of language, is a category of privileged people. They are not the ones to say that privilege is unworthy to be desired. They don't think so and, in any case, it would be indecent for them to say it.

Many indispensable truths, which could save men, go unspoken for reasons of this kind; those who could utter them cannot formulate them and those who could formulate them cannot utter them. If politics were taken seriously, finding a remedy for this would be one of its more urgent problems.

In an unstable society the privileged have a bad conscience. Some of them hide it behind a defiant air and say to the masses: 'It is quite appropriate that I should possess privileges which you are denied.' Others benevolently profess: 'I claim for all of you an equal share in the privileges I enjoy.'

The first attitude is odious. The second is silly, and also too easy.

Both of them equally encourage the people down the road of evil, away from their true and unique good, which they do not possess, but to which, in a sense, they are so close. They are far closer than those who bestow pity on them to an authentic good, which could be a source of beauty and truth and joy and fulfilment. But since they have not reached it and do not know how to, this good might as well be infinitely far away. Those who speak for the people and to them are incapable of understanding either their distress or what an overflowing good is almost within their reach. And, for the people, it is indispensable to be understood.

Affliction is by its nature inarticulate. The afflicted silently beseech to be given the words to express themselves. There are times when they are given none; but there are also times when they are given words, but ill-chosen ones, because those who choose them know nothing of the affliction they would interpret.

Usually, they are far removed from it by the circumstances of their life; but even if they are in close contact with it or have recently experienced it themselves, they are still remote from it because they put it at a distance at the first possible moment.

Thought revolts from contemplating affliction, to the same degree that living flesh recoils from death. A stag advancing voluntarily step by step to offer itself to the teeth of a pack of hounds is about as probable as an act of attention directed towards a real affliction, which is close at hand, on the part of a mind which is free to avoid it.

But that which is indispensable to the good and is impossible naturally is always possible supernaturally.

Supernatural good is not a sort of supplement to natural good, as we are told, with support from Aristotle, for our greater comfort. It would be nice if this were true, but it is not. In all the crucial problems of human existence the only choice is between supernatural good on the one hand and evil on the other.

To put into the mouth of the afflicted words from the vocabulary of middle values, such as democracy, rights, personality, is to offer them something which can bring them no good and will inevitably do them much harm.

These notions do not dwell in heaven; they hang in the middle air, and for this very reason they cannot root themselves in earth.

It is the light falling continually from heaven which alone gives a tree the energy to send powerful roots deep into the earth. The tree is really rooted in the sky.

It is only what comes from heaven that can make a real impress on the earth.

In order to provide an armour for the afflicted, one must put into their mouths only those words whose rightful abode is in heaven, beyond heaven, in the other world. There is no fear of its being impossible. Affliction disposes the soul to welcome and avidly drink in everything which comes from there. For these products it is not consumers but producers who are in short supply.

The test for suitable words is easily recognized and applied. The afflicted are overwhelmed with evil and starving for good. The only words suitable for them are those which express nothing but good, in its pure state. It is easy to discriminate. Words which can be associated with something signifying an evil are alien to pure good. We are criticizing a man when we say: 'He puts his person forward; therefore the person is alien to good. We can speak of an abuse of democracy; therefore democracy is alien to good. To possess a right implies the possibility of making good or bad use of it; therefore rights are alien to good. On the other hand, it is always and everywhere good to fulfil an obligation. Truth, beauty, justice, compassion are always and everywhere good.

For the aspirations of the afflicted, if we wish to be sure of using the right words, all that is necessary is to confine ourselves to those words and phrases which always, everywhere, in all circumstances express only the good.

This is one of the only two services which can be rendered to the afflicted with words. The other is to find the words which express the truth of their affliction, the words which can give resonance, through the crust of external circumstances, to the cry which is always inaudible: 'Why am I being hurt?'

For this, they cannot count upon men of talent, personality, celebrity, or even genius in the sense in which the word is usually employed, which assimilates it to talent. They can count only upon men of the very highest genius: the poet of the *Iliad*, Aeschylus, Sophocles, Shakespeare as he was when he wrote *Lear*, or Racine when he wrote *Phédre*. There are not very many of them.

But there are many human beings only poorly or moderately endowed by nature, who seem infinitely inferior not merely to Homer, Aeschylus, Sophocles, Shakespeare, and Racine but also to Virgil, Corneille, and Hugo, but who nevertheless inhabit the realm of impersonal good where the latter poets never set foot.

A village idiot in the literal sense of the word, if he really loves truth, is infinitely superior to Aristotle in his thought, even though he never utters anything but inarticulate murmurs. He is infinitely closer to Plato than Aristotle ever was. He has genius, while only the word talent applies to Aristotle. If a fairy offered to change his destiny for one resembling Aristotle's he would be wise to refuse unhesitatingly. But he does not know this. And nobody tells him. Everybody tells him the contrary. But he must be told. Idiots, men without talent, men whose talent is average or only a little more, must be encouraged if they possess genius. We need not be afraid of making them proud, because love of truth is always accompanied by humility. Real genius is nothing else but the supernatural virtue of humility in the domain of thought.

What is needed is to cherish the growth of genius, with a warm and tender respect, and not, as the men of 1789 proposed, to encourage the flowering of talents. For it is only heroes of real purity, the saints and geniuses, who can help the afflicted. But the help is obstructed by a screen which is formed between the two by the men of talent, intelligence, energy, character, or strong personality. The screen must not be damaged, but put aside as gently and imperceptibly as possible. The far more dangerous screen of the collective must be broken by abolishing every part of our institutions and customs which harbours the party spirit in any form whatsoever. Neither a personality nor a party is ever responsive either to truth or to affliction.

There is a natural alliance between truth and affliction, because both of them are mute suppliants, eternally condemned to stand speechless in our presence.

Just as a vagrant accused of stealing a carrot from a field stands before a comfortably seated judge who keeps up an elegant flow of queries, comments and witticisms while the accused is unable to stammer a word, so truth stands before an intelligence which is concerned with the elegant manipulation of opinions.

It is always language that formulates opinions, even when there are no words spoken. The natural faculty called intelligence is concerned with opinion and language. Language expresses relations; but it expresses only a few, because its operation needs time. When it is confused and vague, without precision or order, when the speaker or listener is deficient in the power of holding a thought in his mind, then language is empty or almost empty of any real relational content. When it is perfectly clear, precise, rigorous, ordered, when it is addressed to a mind which is capable of keeping a thought present while it adds another to it and of keeping them both present while it adds a third, and so on, then in such a case language can hold a fairly rich content of relations. But like all wealth, this relative wealth is abject poverty compared with the perfection which alone is desirable.

At the very best, a mind enclosed in language is in prison. It is limited to the number of relations which words can make simultaneously present to it; and remains in ignorance of thoughts which involve the combination of a greater number. These thoughts are outside language, they are unformulable, although they are perfectly rigorous and clear and although every one of the relations they involve is capable of precise expression in words. So the mind moves in a closed space of partial truth, which may be larger or smaller, without ever being able so much as to glance at what is outside.

If a captive mind is unaware of being in prison, it is living in error. If it has recognized the fact, even for the tenth of a second, and then quickly forgotten it in order to avoid suffering, it is living in falsehood. Men of the most brilliant intelligence can be born, live, and die in error and falsehood. In them, intelligence is neither a good, nor even an asset. The difference between more or less intelligent men is like the difference between criminals condemned to life imprisonment in smaller or larger cells. The intelligent man who is proud of his intelligence is like a condemned man who is proud of his large cell.

A man whose mind feels that it is captive would prefer to blind himself to the fact. But if he hates falsehood, he will not do so; and in that case he will have to suffer a lot. He will beat his head against the wall until he faints. He will come to again and look with terror at the wall, until one day he begins afresh to beat his head against it; and once again he will faint. And so on endlessly and without hope. One day he will wake up on the other side of the wall.

Perhaps he is still in a prison, although a larger one. No matter. He has found the key; he knows the secret which breaks down every wall. He has passed beyond what men call intelligence, into the beginning of wisdom.

The mind which is enclosed within language can possess only opinions. The mind which has learned to grasp thoughts which are inexpressible because of the number of relations they combine, although they are more rigorous and clearer than anything that can be expressed in the most precise language, such a mind has reached the point where it already dwells in truth. It possesses certainty and unclouded faith. And it matters little whether its original intelligence was great or small, whether its prison cell was narrow or wide. All that matters is that it has come to the end of its intelligence, such as it was, and has passed beyond it. A village idiot is as close to truth as a child prodigy. The one and the other are separated from it only by a wall. But the only way into truth is through one's own annihilation; through dwelling a long time in a state of extreme and total humiliation.

It is the same barrier which keeps us from understanding affliction. Just as truth is a different thing from opinion, so affliction is a different thing from suffering. Affliction is a device for pulverizing the soul; the man who falls into it is like a workman who gets caught up in a machine. He is no longer a man but a torn and bloody rag on the teeth of a cogwheel.

The degree and type of suffering which constitutes affliction in the strict sense of the word varies greatly with different people. It depends chiefly upon the amount of vitality they start with and upon their attitude towards suffering.

Human thought is unable to acknowledge the reality of affliction. To acknowledge the reality of affliction means saying to oneself: 'I may lose at any moment, through the play of circumstances over which I have no control, anything whatsoever that I possess, including those things which are so intimately mine that I consider them as being myself. There is nothing that I might not lose. It could happen at any moment that what I am might be abolished and replaced by anything whatsoever of the filthiest and most contemptible sort.'

To be aware of this in the depth of one's soul is to experience non-being. It is the state of extreme and total humiliation which is also the condition for passing over into truth. It is a death of the soul. This is why the naked spectacle of affliction makes the soul shudder as the flesh shudders at the proximity of death.

We think piously of the dead when we evoke them in memory, or when we walk among graves, or when we see them decently laid out on a bed. But the sight of corpses lying about as on a battlefield can sometimes be both sinister and grotesque. It arouses horror. At the stark sight of death, the flesh recoils.

When affliction is seen vaguely from a distance, either physical or mental, so that it can be confused with simple suffering, it inspires in generous souls a tender feeling of pity. But if by chance it is suddenly revealed to them in all its nakedness as a corrosive force, a mutilation or leprosy of the soul, then people shiver and recoil. The afflicted themselves feel the same shock of horror at their own condition.

To listen to someone is to put oneself in his place while he is speaking. To put oneself in the place of someone whose soul is corroded by affliction, or in near danger of it, is to annihilate oneself. It is more difficult than suicide would be for a happy child. Therefore the afflicted are not listened to. They are like someone whose tongue has been cut out and who occasionally forgets the fact. When they move their lips no ear perceives any sound. And they themselves soon sink into impotence in the use of language, because of the certainty of not being heard.

That is why there is no hope for the vagrant as he stands before the magistrate. Even if, through his stammerings, he should utter a cry to pierce the soul, neither the magistrate nor the public will hear it. His cry is mute. And the afflicted are nearly always equally deaf to one another; and each of them, constrained by the general indifference, strives by means of self-delusion or forgetfulness to become deaf to his own self.

Only by the supernatural working of grace can a soul pass through its own annihilation to the place where alone it can get the sort of attention which can attend to truth and to affliction. It is the same attention which listens to both of them. The name of this intense, pure, disinterested, gratuitous, generous attention is love.

Because affliction and truth need the same kind of attention before they can be heard, the spirit of justice and the spirit of truth are one. The spirit of justice and truth is nothing else but a certain kind of attention, which is pure love.

Thanks to an eternal and providential decree, everything produced by a man in every sphere, when he is ruled by the spirit of justice and truth, is endowed with the radiance of beauty.

Beauty is the supreme mystery of this world. It is a gleam which attracts the attention and yet does nothing to sustain it. Beauty always promises, but never gives anything; it stimulates hunger but has no nourishment for the part of the soul which looks in this world for sustenance. It feeds only the part of the soul that gazes. While exciting desire, it makes clear that there is nothing in it to be desired, because the one thing we want is that it should not change. If one does not seek means to evade the exquisite anguish it inflicts, then desire is gradually transformed into love; and one begins to acquire the faculty of pure and disinterested attention.

In proportion to the hideousness of affliction is the supreme beauty of its true representation. Even in recent times one can point to *Phédre, L'Ecole des femmes, Lear,* and the poems of Villon; but far better examples are the plays of Aeschylus and Sophocles, and far better still, the *Iliad,* the book of Job and certain folk poems; and far beyond these again are the accounts of the Passion in the Gospels. The radiance of beauty illumines affliction with the light of the spirit of justice and love, which is the only light by which human thought can confront affliction and report the truth of it.

And it sometimes happens that a fragment of inexpressible truth is reflected in words which, although they cannot hold the truth that inspired them, have nevertheless so perfect a formal correspondence with it that every mind seeking that truth finds support in them. Whenever this happens a gleam of beauty illumines the words.

Everything which originates from pure love is lit with the radiance of beauty.

Beauty can be perceived, though very dimly and mixed with many false substitutes, within the cell where all human thought is at first imprisoned. And upon her rest all the hopes of truth and justice, with tongue cut out. She, too, has no language; she does not speak; she says nothing. But she has a voice to cry out. She cries out and points to truth and justice who are dumb, like a dog who barks to bring people to his master lying unconscious in the snow.

Justice, truth, and beauty are sisters and comrades. With three such beautiful words we have no need to look for any others.

Justice consists in seeing that no harm is done to men. Whenever a man cries inwardly: 'Why am I being hurt?' harm is being done to him. He is often mistaken when he tries to define the harm, and why and by whom it is being inflicted on him. But the cry itself is infallible.

The other cry, which we hear so often: 'Why has somebody else got more than I have?', refers to rights. We must learn to distinguish between the two cries and to do all that is possible, as gently as possible, to hush the second one, with the help of a code of justice, regular tribunals, and the police. Minds capable of solving problems of this kind can be formed in a law school.

But the cry 'Why am I being hurt?' raises quite different problems, for which the spirit of truth, justice, and love is indispensable.

In every soul the cry to be delivered from evil is incessant. The Lord's Prayer addresses it to God. But God has power to deliver from evil only the eternal part of the soul of those who have made real and direct contact with him. The rest of the soul, and the entire soul of whoever has not received the grace of real and direct contact with God, is at the mercy of men's caprice and the hazards of circumstance.

Therefore it is for men to see that men are preserved from harm.

When harm is done to a man, real evil enters into him; not merely pain and suffering, but the actual horror of evil. Just as men have the power of transmitting good to one another, so they have the power to transmit evil. One may transmit evil to a human being by flattering him or giving him comforts and pleasures; but most often men transmit evil to other men by doing them harm.

Nevertheless, eternal wisdom does not abandon the soul entirely to the mercy of chance and men's caprice. The harm inflicted on a man by a wound from outside sharpens his thirst for the good and thus there automatically arises the possibility of a cure. If the wound is deep, the thirst is for good in its purest form. The part of the soul which cries 'Why am I being hurt?' is on the deepest level and even in the most corrupt of men it remains from earliest infancy perfectly intact and totally innocent.

To maintain justice and preserve men from all harm means first of all to prevent harm being done to them. For those to whom harm has been done, it means to efface the material consequences by putting them in a place where the wound, if it is not too deep, may be cured naturally by a spell of well-being. But for those in whom the wound is a laceration of the soul it means further, and above all, to offer them good in its purest form to assuage their thirst.

Sometimes it may be necessary to inflict harm in

order to stimulate this thirst before assuaging it, and that is what punishment is for. Men who are so estranged from the good that they seek to spread evil everywhere can only be reintegrated with the good by having harm inflicted upon them. This must be done until the completely innocent part of their soul awakens with the surprised cry 'Why am I being hurt?' The innocent part of the criminal's soul must then be fed to make it grow until it becomes able to judge and condemn his past crimes and at last, by the help of grace, to forgive them. With this the punishment is completed; the criminal has been reintegrated with the good and should be publicly and solemnly reintegrated with society.

That is what punishment is. Even capital punishment, although it excludes reintegration with society in the literal sense, should be the same thing. Punishment is solely a method of procuring pure good for men who do not desire it. The art of punishing is the art of awakening in a criminal, by pain or even death, the desire for pure good.

But we have lost all idea of what punishment is. We are not aware that its purpose is to procure good for a man. For us it stops short with the infliction of harm. That is why there is one, and only one, thing in modern society more hideous than crime – namely, repressive justice.

To make the idea of repressive justice the main motive of war or revolt is inconceivably dangerous. It is necessary to use fear as a deterrent against the criminal activity of cowards; but that repressive justice, as we ignorantly conceive it today, should be made the motive of heroes is appalling.

All talk of chastisement, punishment, retribution or punitive justice nowadays always refers solely to the basest kind of revenge.

The treasure of suffering and violent death, which Christ chose for himself and which he so often offers to those he loves, means so little to us that we throw it to those whom we least esteem, knowing that they will make nothing of it and having no intention of helping them to discover its value.

For criminals, true punishment; for those whom affliction has bitten deep into the soul, such help as may bring them to quench their thirst at the supernatural springs; for everyone else, some well-being, a great deal of beauty, and protection from those who would harm him; in every sphere, a strict curb upon the chatter of lies, propaganda, and opinion, and the encouragement of a silence in which truth can germinate and grow; this is what is due to men.

To ensure that they get it, we can only count upon those who have passed beyond a certain barrier, and it may be objected that they are too few in number. Probably there are not many of them, but they are no object for statistics, because most of them are hidden. Pure good from heaven only reaches the earth in imperceptible quantities, whether in the individual soul or in society. The grain of mustard seed is 'the least of all seeds'. Persephone ate only one grain of the pomegranate. A pearl buried deep in a field is not visible; neither is the yeast in dough.

But just as the catalysts or bacteria, such as yeast, operate by their mere presence in chemical reactions, so in human affairs the invisible seed of pure good is decisive when it is put in the right place.

How is it to be put there?

Much could be done by those whose function it is to advise the public what to praise, what to admire, what to hope and strive and seek for. It would be a great advance if even a few of these makers of opinion were to resolve in their hearts to eschew absolutely and without exception everything that is not pure good, perfection, truth, justice, love.

It would be an even greater advance if the majority of those who possess today some fragments of spiritual authority were aware of their obligation never to hold up for human aspiration anything but the real good in its perfect purity.

By the power of words we always mean their power of illusion and error. But, thanks to a providential arrangement, there are certain words which possess, in themselves, when properly used, a virtue which illumines and lifts up towards the good. These are the words which refer to an absolute perfection which we cannot conceive. Since the proper use of these words involves not trying to make them fit any conception, it is in the words themselves, as words, that the power to enlighten and draw upward resides. What they express is beyond our conception.

God and *truth* are such words; also *justice, love* and *good*.

It is dangerous to use words of this kind. They are like an ordeal. To use them legitimately one must avoid referring them to anything humanly conceivable and at the same time one must associate with them ideas and actions which are derived solely and directly from the light which they shed. Otherwise, everyone quickly recognizes them for lies.

They are uncomfortable companions. Words like *right, democracy* and *person* are more accommodating and are therefore naturally preferred by even the best intentioned of those who assume public functions. Public functions have no other meaning except the possibility of doing good to men, and those who assume them with good intentions do in fact want to procure good for their contemporaries; but they usually make the mistake of thinking they can begin by getting it at bargain prices.

Words of the middle region, such as *right, democracy, person,* are valid in their own region, which is that of ordinary institutions. But for the sustaining inspiration of which all institutions are, as it were, the projection, a different language is needed.

The subordination of the person to the collectivity is in the nature of things, like the inferiority of a gram to a kilogram on the scales. But there can be a scales on which the gram outweighs the kilogram. It is only necessary for one arm to be more than a thousand times as long as the other. The law of equilibrium easily overcomes an inequality of weight. But the lesser will never outweigh the greater unless the relation between them is regulated by the law of equilibrium.

In the same way, there is no guarantee for democracy, or for the protection of the person against the collectivity, without a disposition of public life relating it to the higher good which is impersonal and unrelated to any political form.

It is true that the word 'person' is often applied to God. But in the passage where Christ offers God himself as an example to men of the perfection which they are told to achieve, he uses not only the image of a person but also, above all, that of an impersonal order: 'That ye may be like the children of your Father which is in heaven; for he maketh his sun to rise on the evil and on the good, and sendeth rain on the just and on the unjust.'

Justice, truth, and beauty are the image in our world of this impersonal and divine order of the universe. Nothing inferior to them is worthy to be the inspiration of men who accept the fact of death.

Above those institutions which are concerned with protecting rights and persons and democratic freedoms, others must be invented for the purpose of exposing and abolishing everything in contemporary life which buries the soul under injustice, lies, and ugliness.

They must be invented, for they are unknown, and it is impossible to doubt that they are indispensable.

The Needs of the Soul

The notion of obligations comes before that of rights, which is subordinate and relative to the former. A right is not effectual by itself, but only in relation to the obligation to which it corresponds, the effective exercise of a right springing not from the individual who possesses it, but from other men who consider themselves as being under a certain obligation towards him. Recognition of an obligation makes it effectual. An obligation which goes unrecognized by anybody loses none of the full force of its existence. A right which goes unrecognized by anybody is not worth very much.

It makes nonsense to say that men have, on the one hand, rights, and on the other hand, obligations. Such words only express differences in point of view. The actual relationship between the two is as between object and subject. A man, considered in isolation, only has duties, amongst which are certain duties towards himself. Other men, seen from his point of view, only have rights. He, in his turn, has rights, when seen from the point of view of other men, who recognize that they have obligations towards him. A man left alone in the universe would have no rights whatever, but he would have obligations.

The notion of rights, being of an objective order, is inseparable from the notions of existence and reality. This becomes apparent when the obligation descends to the realm of fact; consequently, it always involves to a certain extent the taking into account of actual given states and particular situations. Rights are always found to be related to certain conditions. Obligations alone remain independent of conditions. They belong to a realm situated above all conditions, because it is situated above this world.

The men of 1789 did not recognize the existence of such a realm. All they recognized was the one on the human plane. That is why they started off with the idea of rights. But at the same time they wanted to postulate absolute principles. This contradiction caused them to tumble into a confusion of language and ideas which is largely responsible for the present political and social confusion. The realm of what is eternal, universal, unconditioned is other than the one conditioned by facts, and different ideas hold sway there, ones which are related to the most secret recesses of the human soul.

Obligations are only binding on human beings. There are no obligations for collectivities, as such. But they exist for all human beings who constitute, serve, command or represent a collectivity, in that part of their existence which is related to the collectivity as in that part which is independent of it.

All human beings are bound by identical obligations, although these are performed in different ways according to particular circumstances. No human being, whoever he may be, under whatever circumstances, can escape them without being guilty of crime; save where there are two genuine obligations which are in fact incompatible, and a man is forced to sacrifice one of them.

The imperfections of a social order can be measured by the number of situations of this kind it harbours within itself.

But even in such a case, a crime is committed if the obligation so sacrificed is not merely sacrificed in fact, but its existence denied into the bargain.

The object of any obligation, in the realm of human affairs, is always the human being as such. There exists an obligation towards every human being for the sole reason that he or she *is* a human being, without any other condition requiring to be fulfilled, and even without any recognition of such obligation on the part of the individual concerned.

This obligation is not based upon any *de facto* situation, nor upon jurisprudence, customs, social structure, relative state of forces, historical heritage, or presumed historical orientation; for no *de facto* situation is able to create an obligation.

This obligation is not based upon any convention; for all conventions are liable to be modified according to the wishes of the contracting parties, whereas in this case no change in the mind and will of Man can modify anything whatsoever.

This obligation is an eternal one. It is coextensive

with the eternal destiny of human beings. Only human beings have an eternal destiny. Human collectivities have not got one. Nor are there, in regard to the latter, any direct obligations of an eternal nature. Duty towards the human being as such – that alone is eternal.

This obligation is an unconditional one. If it is founded on something, that something, whatever it is, does not form part of our world. In our world, it is not founded on anything at all. It is the one and only obligation in connection with human affairs that is not subject to any condition.

This obligation has no foundation, but only a verification in the common consent accorded by the universal conscience. It finds expression in some of the oldest written texts which have come down to us. It is recognized by everybody without exception in every single case where it is not attacked as a result of interest or passion. And it is in relation to it that we measure our progress.

The recognition of this obligation is expressed in a confused and imperfect form, that is, more or less imperfect according to the particular case, by what are called positive rights. To the extent to which positive rights are in contradiction with it, to that precise extent is their origin an illegitimate one.

Although this eternal obligation is coextensive with the eternal destiny of the human being, this destiny is not its direct motive. A human being's eternal destiny cannot be the motive of any obligation, for it is not subordinate to external actions.

The fact that a human being possesses an eternal destiny imposes only one obligation: respect. The obligation is only performed if the respect is effectively expressed in a real, not a fictitious, way; and this can only be done through the medium of Man's earthly needs.

On this point, the human conscience has never varied. Thousands of years ago, the Egyptians believed that no soul could justify itself after death unless it could say: 'I have never let anyone suffer from hunger.' All Christians know they are liable to hear Christ himself say to them one day: 'I was an hungered, and ye gave me no meat.' Everyone looks on progress as being, in the first place, a transition to a state of human society in which people will not suffer from hunger. To no matter whom the question may be put in general terms, nobody is of the opinion that any man is innocent if, possessing food himself in abundance and finding someone on his doorstep three parts dead from hunger, he brushes past without giving him anything.

So it is an eternal obligation towards the human being not to let him suffer from hunger when one has the chance of coming to his assistance. This obligation being the most obvious of all, it can serve as a model on which to draw up the list of eternal duties towards each human being. In order to be absolutely correctly made out, this list ought to proceed from the example just given by way of analogy.

Consequently, the list of obligations towards the human being should correspond to the list of such human needs as are vital, analogous to hunger.

Among such needs, there are some which are physical, like hunger itself. They are fairly easy to enumerate. They are concerned with protection against violence, housing, clothing, heating, hygiene and medical attention in case of illness. There are others which have no connection with the physical side of life, but are concerned with its moral side. Like the former, however, they are earthly, and are not directly related, so far as our intelligence is able to perceive, to the eternal destiny of Man. They form, like our physical needs, a necessary condition of our life on this earth. Which means to say that if they are not satisfied, we fall little by little into a state more or less resembling death, more or less akin to a purely vegetative existence.

They are much more difficult to recognize and to enumerate than are the needs of the body. But everyone recognizes that they exist. All the different forms of cruelty which a conqueror can exercise over a subject population, such as massacre, mutilation, organized famine, enslavement or large-scale deportation, are generally considered to be measures of a like description, even though a man's liberty or his native land are not physical necessities. Everyone knows that there are forms of cruelty which can injure a man's life without injuring his body. They are such as deprive him of a certain form of food necessary to the life of the soul.

Obligations, whether unconditional or relative, eternal or changing, direct or indirect with regard to human affairs, all stem, without exception, from the vital needs of the human being. Those which do not directly concern this, that or the other specific human being all exist to serve requirements which, with respect to Man, play a role analogous to food.

We owe a cornfield respect, not because of itself, but because it is food for mankind.

In the same way, we owe our respect to a collectivity, of whatever kind – country, family, or any other – not for itself, but because it is food for a certain number of human souls.

Actually, this obligation makes different attitudes, actions necessary according to different situations. But, taken by itself, it is absolutely identical for everybody. More particularly is this so for all those outside such a collectivity.

The degree of respect owing to human collectivities is a very high one, for several reasons.

To start with, each is unique, and, if destroyed, cannot be replaced. One sack of corn can always be substituted for another sack of corn. The food which a collectivity supplies for the souls of those who form part of it has no equivalent in the entire universe.

Secondly, because of its continuity, a collectivity is already moving forward into the future. It contains food, not only for the souls of the living, but also for the souls of beings yet unborn which are to come into the world during the immediately succeeding centuries.

Lastly, due to this same continuity, a collectivity has its roots in the past. It constitutes the sole agency for preserving the spiritual treasures accumulated by the dead, the sole transmitting agency by means of which the dead can speak to the living. And the sole earthly reality which is directly connected with the eternal destiny of Man is the irradiating light of those who have managed to become fully conscious of this destiny, transmitted from generation to generation.

Because of all this, it may happen that the obligation towards a collectivity which is in danger reaches the point of entailing a total sacrifice. But it does not follow from this that collectivities are superior to human beings. It sometimes happens, too, that the obligation to go to the help of a human being in distress makes a total sacrifice necessary, without that implying any superiority on the part of the individual so helped.

A peasant may, under certain circumstances, be under the necessity, in order to cultivate his land, of risking exhaustion, illness or even death. But all the time he will be conscious of the fact that it is solely a matter of bread.

Similarly, even when a total sacrifice is required, no more is owed to any collectivity whatever than a respect analogous to the one owed to food.

It very often happens that the roles are reversed. There are collectivities which, instead of serving as food, do just the opposite: they devour souls. In such cases, the social body is diseased, and the first duty is to attempt a cure; in certain circumstances, it may be necessary to have recourse to surgical methods.

With regard to this matter, too, the obligation for

those inside as for those outside the collectivity is an identical one.

It also happens that a collectivity supplies insufficient food for the souls of those forming part of it. In that case, it has to be improved.

Finally, there are dead collectivities which, without devouring souls, don't nourish them either. If it is absolutely certain that they are well and truly dead, that it isn't just a question of a temporary lethargy, then and only then should they be destroyed.

The first thing to be investigated is what are those needs which are for the life of the soul; what the needs in the way of food, sleep and warmth are for the life of the body. We must try to enumerate and define them.

They must never be confused with desires, whims, fancies and vices. We must also distinguish between what is fundamental and what is fortuitous. Man requires, not rice or potatoes, but food; not wood or coal, but heating. In the same way, for the needs of the soul, we must recognize the different, but equivalent, sorts of satisfaction which cater for the same requirements. We must also distinguish between the soul's foods and poisons which, for a time, can give the impression of occupying the place of the former.

The lack of any such investigation forces governments, even when their intentions are honest, to act sporadically and at random.

Below are offered a few indications.

ORDER

The first of the soul's needs, the one which touches most nearly its eternal destiny, is order; that is to say, a texture of social relationships such that no one is compelled to violate imperative obligations in order to carry out other ones. It is only where this, in fact, occurs that external circumstances have any power to inflict spiritual violence on the soul. For he for whom the threat of death or suffering is the one thing standing in the way of the performance of an obligation can overcome this disability, and will only suffer in his body. But he who finds that circumstances, in fact, render the various acts necessitated by a series of strict obligations incompatible with one another is, without being able to offer any resistance thereto, made to suffer in his love of good.

At the present time, a very considerable amount of confusion and incompatibility exists between obligations.

Whoever acts in such a way as to increase this incompatibility is a troublemaker. Whoever acts in such a way as to diminish it is an agent of order. Whoever, so as to simplify problems, denies the existence of certain obligations has, in his heart, made a compact with crime.

Unfortunately, we possess no method for diminishing this incompatibility. We cannot even be sure that the idea of an order in which all obligations would be compatible with one another isn't itself a fiction. When duty descends to the level of facts, so many independent relationships are brought into play that incompatibility seems far more likely than compatibility.

Nevertheless, we have every day before us the example of a universe in which an infinite number of independent mechanical actions concur so as to produce an order that, in the midst of variations, remains fixed. Furthermore, we love the beauty of the world, because we sense behind it the presence of something akin to that wisdom we should like to possess to slake our thirst for good.

In a minor degree, really beautiful works of art are examples of *ensembles* in which independent factors concur, in a manner impossible to understand, so as to form a unique thing of beauty.

Finally, a consciousness of the various obligations always proceeds from a desire for good which is unique, unchanging and identical with itself for every man, from the cradle to the grave. This desire, perpetually stirring in the depths of our being, makes it impossible for us ever to resign ourselves to situations in which obligations are incompatible with one another. Either we have recourse to lying in order to forget their existence, or we struggle blindly to extricate ourselves from them.

The contemplation of veritable works of art, and much more still that of the beauty of the world, and again much more that of the unrealized good to which we aspire, can sustain us in our efforts to think continually about that human order which should be the subject uppermost in our minds.

The great instigators of violence have encouraged themselves with the thought of how blind, mechanical force is sovereign throughout the whole universe.

By looking at the world with keener senses than theirs, we shall find a more powerful encouragement in the thought of how these innumerable blind forces are limited, made to balance one against the other, brought to form a united whole by something which we do not understand, but which we call beauty.

If we keep ever-present in our minds the idea of a veritable human order, if we think of it as of something to which a total sacrifice is due should the need arise, we shall be in a similar position to that of a man travelling, without a guide, through the night, but continually thinking of the direction he wishes to follow. Such a traveller's way is lit by a great hope.

Order is the first need of all; it even stands above all needs properly so-called. To be able to conceive it, we must know what the other needs are.

The first characteristic which distinguishes needs from desires, fancies or vices, and foods from gluttonous repasts or poisons, is that needs are limited, in exactly the same way as are the foods corresponding to them. A miser never has enough gold, but the time comes when any man provided with an unlimited supply of bread finds he has had enough. Food brings satiety. The same applies to the soul's foods.

The second characteristic, closely connected with the first, is that needs are arranged in antithetical pairs and have to combine together to form a balance. Man requires food, but also an interval between his meals; he requires warmth and coolness, rest and exercise. Likewise in the case of the soul's needs.

What is called the golden mean actually consists in satisfying neither the one nor the other of two contrary needs. It is a caricature of the genuinely balanced state in which contrary needs are each fully satisfied in turn.

LIBERTY

One of the indispensable foods of the human soul is liberty. Liberty, taking the word in its concrete sense, consists in the ability to choose. We must understand by that, of course, a real ability. Wherever men are living in community, rules imposed in the common interest must necessarily limit the possibilities of choice.

But a greater or lesser degree of liberty does not depend on whether the limits set are wider or narrower. Liberty attains its plenitude under conditions which are less easily gauged.

Rules should be sufficiently sensible and sufficiently straightforward so that anyone who so desires and is blessed with average powers of application may be able to understand, on the one hand the useful ends they serve, and on the other hand the actual necessities which have brought about their institution. They should emanate from a source of authority which is not looked upon as strange or hostile, but loved as something belonging to those placed under its direction. They should be sufficiently stable, general and limited in number for the mind to be able to grasp them once and for all, and not find itself brought up against them every time a decision has to be made.

Under these conditions, the liberty of men of good-will, though limited in the sphere of action, is complete in that of conscience. For, having incorporated the rules into their own being, the prohibited possibilities no longer present themselves to the mind, and have not to be rejected. Just as the habit, formed by education, of not eating disgusting or dangerous things is not felt by the normal man to be any limitation of his liberty in the domain of food. Only a child feels such a limitation.

Those who are lacking in goodwill or who remain adolescent are never free under any form of society.

When the possibilities of choice are so wide as to injure the commonweal, men cease to enjoy liberty. For they must either seek refuge in irresponsibility, puerility and indifference – a refuge where the most they can find is boredom – or feel themselves weighed down by responsibility at all times for fear of causing harm to others. Under such circumstances, men, believing, wrongly, that they are in possession of liberty, and feeling that they get no enjoyment out of it, end up by thinking that liberty is not a good thing.

OBEDIENCE

Obedience is a vital need of the human soul. It is of two kinds: obedience to established rules and obedience to human beings looked upon as leaders. It presupposes consent, not in regard to every single order received, but the kind of consent that is given once and for all, with the sole reservation, in case of need, that the demands of conscience be satisfied.

It requires to be generally recognized, and above all by leaders themselves, that consent and not fear of punishment or hope of reward constitutes, in fact, the mainspring of obedience, so that submission may never be mistaken for servility. It should also be realized that those who command, obey in their turn, and the whole hierarchy should have its face set in the direction of a goal whose importance and even grandeur can be felt by all, from the highest to the lowest.

Obedience being a necessary food of the soul, whoever is definitely deprived of it is ill. Thus, any body politic governed by a sovereign ruler accountable to nobody is in the hands of a sick man.

That is why wherever a man is placed for life at the head of the social organism, he ought to be a symbol and not a ruler, as is the case with the king of England; etiquette ought also to restrict his freedom more narrowly than that of any single man of the people. In this way, the effective rulers, rulers though they be, have somebody over them; on the other hand, they are able to replace each other in unbroken continuity, and consequently to receive, each in his turn, that indispensable amount of obedience due to him.

Those who keep masses of men in subjection by exercising force and cruelty deprive them at once of two vital foods, liberty and obedience; for it is no longer within the power of such masses to accord their inner consent to the authority to which they are subjected. Those who encourage a state of things in which the hope of gain is the principal motive take away from men their obedience, for consent which is its essence is not something which can be sold.

There are any number of signs showing that the men of our age have now for a long time been starved of obedience. But advantage has been taken of the fact to give them slavery.

RESPONSIBILITY

Initiative and responsibility, to feel one is useful and even indispensable, are vital needs of the human soul.

Complete privation from this point of view is the case of the unemployed person, even if he receives assistance to the extent of being able to feed, clothe and house himself. For he represents nothing at all in the economic life of his country, and the voting paper which represents his share in its political life doesn't hold any meaning for him.

The manual labourer is in a scarcely better position.

For this need to be satisfied it is necessary that a man should often have to take decisions in matters great or small affecting interests that are distinct from his own, but in regard to which he feels a personal concern. He also requires to be continually called upon to supply fresh efforts. Finally, he requires to be able to encompass in thought the entire range of activity of the social organism to which he belongs, including branches in connection with which he has never to take a decision or offer any advice. For that, he must be made acquainted with it, be asked to interest himself in it, be brought to feel its value, its utility and, where necessary, its greatness, and be made fully aware of the part he plays in it.

Every social organism, of whatever kind it may be, which does not provide its members with these satisfactions, is diseased and must be restored to health.

In the case of every person of fairly strong character, the need to show initiative goes so far as the need to take command. A flourishing local and regional life, a host of educational activities and youth movements, ought to furnish whoever is able to take advantage of it with the opportunity to command at certain periods of his life.

EQUALITY

Equality is a vital need of the human soul. It consists in a recognition, at once public, general, effective and genuinely expressed in institutions and customs, that the same amount of respect and consideration is due to every human being because this respect is due to the human being as such and is not a matter of degree.

It follows that the inevitable differences among men ought never to imply any difference in the degree of respect. And so that these differences may not be felt to bear such an implication, a certain balance is necessary between equality and inequality.

A certain combination of equality and inequality is formed by equality of opportunity. If no matter who can attain the social rank corresponding to the function he is capable of filling, and if education is sufficiently generalized so that no one is prevented from developing any capacity simply on account of his birth, the prospects are the same for every child. In this way, the prospects for each man are the same as for any other man, both as regards himself when young, and as regards his children later on.

But when such a combination acts alone, and not as one factor amongst other factors, it ceases to constitute a balance and contains great dangers.

To begin with, for a man who occupies an inferior position and suffers from it to know that his position is a result of his incapacity and that everybody is aware of the fact is not any consolation, but an additional motive of bitterness; according to the individual character, some men can thereby be thrown into a state of depression, while others can be encouraged to commit crime.

Then, in social life, a sort of aspirator towards the top is inevitably created. If a descending movement does not come to balance this ascending movement, the social body becomes sick. To the extent to which it is really possible for the son of a farm labourer to become one day a minister, to the same extent should it really be possible for the son of a minister to become one day a farm labourer. This second possibility could never assume any noticeable proportions without a very dangerous degree of social constraint.

This sort of equality, if allowed full play by itself, can make social life fluid to the point of decomposing it.

There are less clumsy methods of combining equality with differentiation. The first is by using proportion. Proportion can be defined as the combination of equality with inequality, and everywhere throughout the universe it is the sole factor making for balance.

Applied to the maintenance of social equilibrium, it would impose on each man burdens corresponding to the power and well-being he enjoys, and corresponding risks in cases of incapacity or neglect. For instance, an employer who is incapable or guilty of an offence against his workmen ought to be made to suffer far more, both in the spirit and in the flesh, than a workman who is incapable or guilty of an offence against his employer. Furthermore, all workmen ought to know that this is so. It would imply, on the one hand, a certain rearrangement with regard to risks, on the other hand, in criminal law, a conception of punishment in which social rank, as an aggravating circumstance, would necessarily play an important part in deciding what the penalty was to be. All the more reason, therefore, why the exercise of important public functions should carry with it serious personal risks.

Another way of rendering equality compatible with differentiation would be to take away as far as possible all quantitative character from differences. Where there is only a difference in kind, not in degree, there is no inequality at all.

By making money the sole, or almost the sole, motive

of all actions, the sole, or almost the sole, measure of all things, the poison of inequality has been introduced everywhere. It is true that this inequality is mobile; it is not attached to persons, for money is made and lost; it is none the less real.

There are two sorts of inequality, each with its corresponding stimulant. A more or less stable inequality, like that of ancient France, produces an idolizing of superiors – not without a mixture of repressed hatred – and a submission to their commands. A mobile, fluid inequality produces a desire to better oneself. It is no nearer to equality than is stable inequality, and is every bit as unwholesome. The Revolution of 1789, in putting forward equality, only succeeded in reality in sanctioning the substitution of one form of inequality for another.

The more equality there is in a society, the smaller is the action of the two stimulants connected with the two forms of inequality, and hence other stimulants are necessary.

Equality is all the greater in proportion as different human conditions are regarded as being, not more nor less than one another, but simply as other. Let us look on the professions of miner and minister simply as two different vocations, like those of poet and mathematician. And let the material hardships attaching to the miner's condition be counted in honour of those who undergo them.

In wartime, if an army is filled with the right spirit, a soldier is proud and happy to be under fire instead of at headquarters; a general is proud and happy to think that the successful outcome of the battle depends on his forethought; and at the same time the soldier admires the general and the general the soldier.

Such a balance constitutes an equality. There would be equality in social conditions if this balance could be found therein. It would mean honouring each human condition with those marks of respect which are proper to it, and are not just a hollow pretence.

HIERARCHISM

Hierarchism is a vital need of the human soul. It is composed of a certain veneration, a certain devotion towards superiors, considered not as individuals, nor in relation to the powers they exercise, but as symbols. What they symbolize is that realm situated high above all men and whose expression in this world is made up of the obligations owed by each man to his fellow-men. A veritable hierarchy presupposes a consciousness on the part of the superiors of this symbolic function and a realization that it forms the only legitimate object of devotion among their subordinates. The effect of true hierarchism is to bring each one to fit himself morally into the place he occupies.

HONOUR

Honour is a vital need of the human soul. The respect due to every human being as such, even if effectively accorded, is not sufficient to satisfy this need, for it is identical for every one and unchanging; whereas honour has to do with a human being considered not simply as such, but from the point of view of his social surroundings. This need is fully satisfied where each of the social organisms to which a human being belongs allows him to share in a noble tradition enshrined in its past history and given public acknowledgement.

For example, for the need of honour to be satisfied in professional life, every profession requires to have some association really capable of keeping alive the memory of all the store of nobility, heroism, probity, generosity and genius spent in the exercise of that profession.

All oppression creates a famine in regard to the need of honour, for the noble traditions possessed by those suffering oppression go unrecognized, through lack of social prestige.

Conquest always has that effect. Vercingetorix was no hero to the Romans. Had France been conquered by the English in the fifteenth century, Joan of Arc would be well and truly forgotten, even to a great extent by us. We now talk about her to the Annamites and the Arabs; but they know very well that here in France we don't allow their heroes and saints to be talked about; therefore the state in which we keep them is an affront to their honour.

Social oppression has the same effects. Guynemer and Mermoz have become part of the public consciousness, thanks to the social prestige of aviation; the sometimes incredible heroism displayed by miners or fishermen barely awakes an echo among miners or fishermen themselves.

Deprivation of honour attains its extreme degree with that total deprivation of respect reserved for certain categories of human beings. In France, this affects, under various forms, prostitutes, ex-convicts, police agents and the sub-proletariat composed of colonial immigrants and natives. Categories of this kind ought not to exist.

Crime alone should place the individual who has committed it outside the social pale, and punishment should bring him back again inside it.

PUNISHMENT

Punishment is a vital need of the human soul. There are two kinds of punishment, disciplinary and penal. The former offers security against failings with which it would be too exhausting to struggle if there were no exterior support. But the most indispensable punishment for the soul is that inflicted for crime. By committing crime, a man places himself, of his own accord, outside the chain of eternal obligations which bind every human being to every other one. Punishment alone can weld him back again; fully so, if accompanied by consent on his part; otherwise only partially so. Just as the only way of showing respect for somebody suffering from hunger is to give him something to eat, so the only way of showing respect for somebody who has placed himself outside the law is to reinstate him inside the law by subjecting him to the punishment ordained by the law.

The need of punishment is not satisfied where, as is generally the case, the penal code is merely a method of exercising pressure through fear.

So that this need may be satisfied, it is above all necessary that everything connected with the penal law should wear a solemn and consecrated aspect; that the majesty of the law should make its presence felt by the court, the police, the accused, the guilty man – even when the case dealt with is of minor importance, provided it entails a possible loss of liberty. Punishment must be an honour. It must not only wipe out the stigma of the crime, but must be regarded as a supplementary form of education, compelling a higher devotion to the public good. The severity of the punishment must also be in keeping with the kind of obligation which has been violated, and not with the interests of public security.

The discredit attaching to the police, the irresponsible conduct of the judiciary, the prison system, the permanent social stigma cast upon ex-convicts, the scale of penalties which provides a much harsher punishment for ten acts of petty larceny than for one rape or certain types of murder, and which even provides punishments for ordinary misfortune – all this makes it impossible for there to exist among us, in France, anything that deserves the name of punishment.

For offences, as for crimes, the relative degree of immunity should increase, not as you go up, but as you go down the social scale. Otherwise the hardships inflicted will be felt to be in the nature of constraints or even abuses of power, and will no longer constitute punishments. Punishment only takes place where the hardship is accompanied at some time or another, even after it is over, and in retrospect, by a feeling of justice. Just as the musician awakens the sense of beauty in us by sounds, so the penal system should know how to awaken the sense of justice in the criminal by the infliction of pain, or even, if need be, of death. And in the same way as we can say of the apprentice who injures himself at his trade, that it is the trade which is getting into *him,* so punishment is a method for getting justice into the soul of the criminal by bodily suffering.

The question of the best means to employ to prevent a conspiracy from arising in high places with the object of obtaining immunity from the law, is one of the most difficult political problems to solve. It can only be solved if there are men whose duty it is to prevent such a conspiracy, and whose situation in life is such that they are not tempted to enter it themselves.

FREEDOM OF OPINION

Freedom of opinion and freedom of association are usually classed together. It is a mistake. Save in the case of natural groupings, association is not a need, but an expedient employed in the practical affairs of life.

On the other hand, complete, unlimited freedom of expression for every sort of opinion, without the least restriction or reserve, is an absolute need on the part of the intelligence. It follows from this that it is a need of the soul, for when the intelligence is ill at ease the whole soul is sick. The nature and limits of the satisfaction corresponding to this need are inscribed in the very structure of the various faculties of the soul. For the same thing can be at once limited and unlimited, just as one can produce the length of a rectangle indefinitely without it ceasing to be limited in width.

In the case of a human being, the intelligence can be exercised in three ways. It can work on technical problems, that is to say, discover means to achieve an already given objective. It can provide light when a choice lies before the will concerning the path to be followed. Finally, it can operate alone, separately from the other faculties, in a purely theoretical speculation where all question of action has been provisionally set aside.

When the soul is in a healthy condition, it is exercised in these three ways in turn, with different degrees of freedom. In the first function, it acts as a servant. In the second function, it acts destructively and requires to be reduced to silence immediately it begins to supply arguments to that part of the soul which, in the case of anyone not in a state of perfection, always places itself on the side of evil. But when it operates alone and separately, it must be in possession of sovereign liberty; otherwise something essential is wanting to the human being.

The same applies in a healthy society. That is why it

would be desirable to create an absolutely free reserve in the field of publication, but in such a way as for it to be understood that the works found therein did not pledge their authors in any way and contained no direct advice for readers. There it would be possible to find, set out in their full force, all the arguments in favour of bad causes. It would be an excellent and salutary thing for them to be so displayed. Anybody could there sing the praises of what he most condemns. It would be publicly recognized that the object of such works was not to define their authors' attitudes *vis-à-vis* the problems of life, but to contribute, by preliminary researches, towards a complete and correct tabulation of data concerning each problem. The law would see to it that their publication did not involve any risk of whatever kind for the author.

On the other hand, publications destined to influence what is called opinion, that is to say, in effect, the conduct of life, constitute acts and ought to be subjected to the same restrictions as are all acts. In other words, they should not cause unlawful harm of any kind to any human being, and above all, should never contain any denial, explicit or implicit, of the eternal obligations towards the human being, once these obligations have been solemnly recognized by law.

The distinction between the two fields, the one which is outside action and the one which forms part of action, is impossible to express on paper in juridical terminology. But that doesn't prevent it from being a perfectly clear one. The separate existence of these two fields is not difficult to establish in fact, if only the will to do so is sufficiently strong.

It is obvious, for example, that the entire daily and weekly press comes within the second field; reviews also, for they all constitute, individually, a focus of radiation in regard to a particular way of thinking; only those which were to renounce this function would be able to lay claim to total liberty.

The same applies to literature. It would solve the argument which arose not long ago on the subject of literature and morals, and which was clouded over by the fact that all the talented people, through professional solidarity, were found on one side, and only fools and cowards on the other.

But the attitude of the fools and cowards was none the less, to a large extent, consistent with the demands of reason. Writers have an outrageous habit of playing a double game. Never so much as in our age have they claimed the role of directors of conscience and exercised it. Actually, during the years immediately preceding the war, no one challenged their right to it except the savants. The position formerly occupied by priests in the moral life of the country was held by physicists and novelists, which is sufficient to gauge the value of our progress. But if somebody called upon writers to render an account of the orientation set by their influence, they barricaded themselves indignantly behind the sacred privilege of art for art's sake.

There is not the least doubt, for example, that André Gide has always known that books like *Les Nourritures*

Terrestres and *Les Caves du Vatican* have exercised an influence on the practical conduct of life of hundreds of young people, and he has been proud of the fact. There is, then, no reason for placing such books behind the inviolable barrier of art for art's sake, and sending to prison a young fellow who pushes somebody off a train in motion. One might just as well claim the privileges of art for art's sake in support of crime. At one time the Surrealists came pretty close to doing so. All that has been repeated by so many idiots *ad nauseam* about the responsibility of our writers in the defeat of France in 1940 is, unfortunately, only too true.

If a writer, thanks to the complete freedom of expression accorded to pure intelligence, publishes written matter which goes contrary to the moral principals recognized by law, and if later on he becomes a notorious focus of influence, it is simple enough to ask him if he is prepared to state publicly that his writings do not express his personal attitude. If he is not prepared to do so, it is simple enough to punish him. If he lies, it is simple enough to discredit him. Moreover, it ought to be recognized that the moment a writer fills a role among the influences directing public opinion, he cannot claim to exercise unlimited freedom. Here again, a juridical definition is impossible; but the facts are not really difficult to discern. There is no reason at all why the sovereignty of the law should be limited to the field of what can be expressed in legal formulae, since that sovereignty is exercised just as well by judgments in equity.

Besides, the need of freedom itself, so essential to the

intellect, calls for a corresponding protection against suggestion, propaganda, influence by means of obsession. These are methods of constraint, a special kind of constraint, not accompanied by fear or physical distress, but which is none the less a form of violence. Modern technique places extremely potent instruments at its service. This constraint is, by its very nature, collective, and human souls are its victims.

Naturally, the State is guilty of crime if it makes use of such methods itself, save in cases where the public safety is absolutely at stake. But it should, furthermore, prevent their use. Publicity, for example, should be rigorously controlled by law and its volume very considerably reduced; it should also be severely prohibited from ever dealing with subjects which belong to the domain of thought.

Likewise, repression could be exercised against the press, radio broadcasts, or anything else of a similar kind, not only for offences against moral principles publicly recognized, but also for baseness of tone and thought, bad taste, vulgarity or a subtly corrupting moral atmosphere. This sort of repression could take place without in any way infringing on freedom of opinion. For instance, a newspaper could be suppressed without the members of its editorial staff losing the right to go on publishing wherever they liked, or even, in the less serious cases, remain associated to carry on the same paper under another name. Only, it would have been publicly branded with infamy and would run the risk of being so again. Freedom of opinion can be claimed solely – and even then with certain reservations – by the journalist, not by the paper; for it is only the journalist who is capable of forming an opinion.

Generally speaking, all problems to do with freedom of expression are clarified if it is posited that this freedom is a need of the intelligence, and that intelligence resides solely in the human being, individually considered. There is no such thing as a collective exercise of the intelligence. It follows that no group can legitimately claim freedom of expression, because no group has the slightest need of it.

In fact the opposite applies. Protection of freedom of thought requires that no group should be permitted by law to express an opinion. For when a group starts having opinions, it inevitably tends to impose them on its members. Sooner or later, these individuals find themselves debarred, with a greater or lesser degree of severity, and on a number of problems of greater or lesser importance, from expressing opinions opposed to those of the group, unless they care to leave it. But a break with any group to which one belongs always involves suffering – at any rate of a sentimental kind. And just as danger, exposure to suffering are healthy and necessary elements in the sphere of action, so are they unhealthy influences in the exercise of the intelligence. A fear, even a passing one, always provokes either a weakening or a tautening, depending on the degree of courage, and that is all that is required to damage the extremely delicate and fragile instrument of precision which constitutes our intelligence. Even friendship is, from this point of view, a great danger. The intelligence is defeated as soon as the expression of one's thoughts is preceded, explicitly or implicitly, by the little word 'we'. And when the light of the intelligence grows dim, it is not very long before the love of good becomes lost.

The immediate, practical solution would be the abolition of political parties. Party strife, as it existed under the Third Republic, is intolerable. The single party, which is, moreover, its inevitable outcome, is the worst evil of all. The only remaining possibility is a public life without parties. Nowadays, such an idea strikes us as a novel and daring proposition. All the better, since something novel is what is wanted. But, in point of fact, it is only going back to the tradition of 1789. In the eyes of the people of 1789, there was literally no other possibility. A public life like ours has been over the course of the last half-century would have seemed to them a hideous nightmare. They would never have believed it possible that a representative of the people should so divest himself of all personal dignity as to allow himself to become the docile member of a party.

Moreover, Rousseau had clearly demonstrated how party strife automatically destroys the Republic. He had foretold its effects. It would be a good thing just now to encourage the reading of the *Contrat Social*. Actually, at the present time, wherever there were political parties, democracy is dead. We all know that the parties in England have a certain tradition, spirit and function making it impossible to compare them to anything else. We all know, besides, that the rival teams in the United States are not political parties. A democracy where public life is made up of strife between political parties is incapable of preventing the formation of a party whose avowed aim is the overthrow of that democracy. If such a democracy brings in discriminatory laws, it cuts its own throat. If it doesn't, it is just as safe as a little bird in front of a snake.

A distinction ought to be drawn between two sorts of associations: those concerned with interests, where organization and discipline would be countenanced up to a certain point, and those concerned with ideas, where such things would be strictly forbidden. Under present conditions, it is a good thing to allow people to group themselves together to defend their interests, in other words, their wage receipts and so forth, and to leave these associations to act within very narrow limits and under the constant supervision of the authorities. But such associations should not be allowed to have anything to do with ideas. Associations in which ideas are being canvassed should be not so much associations as more or less fluid social mediums. When some action is contemplated within them, there is no reason why it need be put into execution by any persons other than those who approve of it.

In the working-class movement, for example, such a distinction would put an end to the present inextricable confusion. In the period before the war, the working-man's attention was being continually pulled in three directions at once. In the first place, by the struggle for higher wages; secondly, by what remained – growing ever feebler, but still showing some signs of life – of the old trade-union spirit of former days, idealist and more or less libertarian in character; and, lastly, by the political parties. Very often, when a strike was on, the workmen who struggled and suffered would have been quite incapable of deciding for themselves whether it was all a matter of wages, a revival of the old trade-union spirit, or a political manoeuvre conducted by a party; and nobody looking on from the outside was in any better position to judge.

That is an impossible state of affairs. When the war broke out, the French trade unions were dead or moribund, in spite of their millions of members – or because of them. They again took on some semblance of life, after a prolonged lethargy, when the Resistance against the invader got under way. That doesn't prove that they are viable. It is perfectly clear that they had been all but destroyed by two sorts of poison, each of which by itself is deadly.

Trade unions cannot flourish if at their meetings the workmen are obsessed by their earnings to the same extent as they are in the factory, when engaged in piece-work. To begin with, because the result is that sort of moral death always brought about by an obsession in regard to money. Next, because the trade union, having become, under present social conditions, a factor continually acting upon the economic life of the country, ends up inevitably by being transformed into a single, compulsory, professional organization, obliged to toe the line in public affairs. It has then been changed into the semblance of a corpse.

Besides, it is no less evident that trade unions cannot live in intimate contact with political parties. There is something resulting from the normal play of mechanical forces which makes such a thing quite impossible. For an analogous reason, moreover, the Socialist Party cannot live side by side with the Communist Party, because the latter's party character is, as it were, marked to a so much greater degree.

Furthermore, the obsession about wages strengthens Communist influence, because questions to do with money, however closely they may affect the majority of men, produce at the same time in all men a sensation of such deadly boredom that it requires to be compensated by the apocalyptic prospect of the Revolution, according to Communist tenets. If the middle classes haven't the same need of an apocalypse, it is because long rows of figures have a poetry, a prestige which tempers in some sort the boredom associated with money; whereas, when money is counted in sixpences, we have boredom in its pure, unadulterated state. Nevertheless, the taste shown by *bourgeois,* both great and small, for Fascism, indicates that, in spite of everything, they too can feel bored.

Under the Vichy Government, single and compulsory professional organizations for workmen have been created. It is a pity that they have been given, according to the modern fashion, the name of corporation, which denotes, in reality, something so very different and so beautiful. But it is a good thing that such dead organizations should be there to take over the dead part of trade-union activity. It would be dangerous to do away with them. It is far better to charge them with the day-to-day business of dealing with wages and what are called immediate demands. As for the political parties, if they were all strictly prohibited in a general atmosphere of liberty, it is to be hoped their underground existence would at any rate be made difficult for them.

In that event, the workmen's trade unions, if they still retain a spark of any real life, could become again, little by little, the expression of working-class thought, the instrument of working-class integrity. According to the traditions of the French working-class movement, which has always looked upon itself as responsible for the whole world, they would concern themselves with everything to do with justice – including, where necessary, questions about wages; but only at long intervals and to rescue human beings from poverty.

Naturally, they would have to be able to exert an influence on professional organizations, according to methods of procedure defined by law.

There would, perhaps, only be advantages to be gained by making it illegal for professional organizations to launch a strike, and allowing trade unions – with certain restrictions – to do so, while at the same time attaching risks to this responsibility, prohibiting any sort of coercion, and safeguarding the continuity of economic life.

As for the lockout, there is no reason why it should not be entirely suppressed.

The authorized existence of associations for promoting ideas could be subject to two conditions. First, that excommunication may not be applied. Recruitment would be voluntary and as a result of personal affinity, without, however, making anybody liable to be invited to subscribe to a collection of assertions crystallized in written form. But once a member had been admitted, he could not be expelled except for some breach of integrity or undermining activities; which latter offence would, moreover, imply the existence of an illegal organization, and consequently expose the offender to a more severe punishment.

This would, in fact, amount to a measure of public safety, experience having shown that totalitarian States are set up by totalitarian parties, and that these totalitarian parties are formed by dint of expulsions for the crime of having an opinion of one's own.

The second condition could be that ideas must really be put into circulation, and tangible proof of such circulation given in the shape of pamphlets, reviews or typed bulletins in which problems of general interest were discussed. Too great a uniformity of opinion would render any such association suspect.

For the rest, all associations for promoting ideas would be authorized to act according as they thought fit, on condition that they didn't break the law or exert any sort of disciplinary pressure on their members.

As regards associations for promoting interests, their control would, in the first place, involve the making of a distinction, namely, that the word 'interest' sometimes expresses a need and at other times something quite different. In the case of a poor working man, interest means food, lodging and heating. For an employer, it means something of a different kind. When the word is taken in its first sense, the action of the authorities should be mainly to stimulate, uphold and defend the interests concerned. When used in its second sense, the action of the authorities should be continually to supervise, limit and, whenever possible, curb the activities of the associations representing such interests. It goes without saying that the severest restrictions and the hardest punishments should be reserved for those which are, by their nature, the most powerful.

What has been called freedom of association has been, in fact, up to now, freedom for associations. But associations have not got to be free; they are instruments, they must be held in bondage. Only the human being is fit to be free.

As regards freedom of thought, it is very nearly true to say that without freedom there *is* no thought. But it is truer still to say that when thought is non-existent, it is non-free into the bargain. There has been a lot of freedom of thought over the past few years, but no thought. Rather like the case of a child who, not having any meat, asks for salt with which to season it.

SECURITY

Security is an essential need of the soul. Security means that the soul is not under the weight of fear or terror, except as the result of an accidental conjunction of circumstances and for brief and exceptional periods. Fear and terror, as permanent states of the soul, are well-nigh mortal poisons, whether they be caused by the threat of unemployment, police persecution, the presence of a foreign conqueror, the probability of invasion, or any other calamity which seems too much for human strength to bear.

The Roman masters used to place a whip in the hall within sight of their slaves, knowing that this spectacle reduced their hearts to that half-dead condition indispensable for slavery. On the other hand, according to the Egyptians, the just man should be able to say after death: 'I never caused anyone any fear.'

Even if permanent fear constitutes a latent state only, so that its painful effects are only rarely experienced directly, it remains always a disease. It is a semi-paralysis of the soul.

RISK

Risk is an essential need of the soul. The absence of risk produces a type of boredom which paralyses in a different way from fear, but almost as much. Moreover, there are certain situations which, involving as they do a diffused anguish without any clearly defined risks, spread the two kinds of disease at once.

Risk is a form of danger which provokes a deliberate reaction; that is to say, it doesn't go beyond the soul's resources to the point of crushing the soul beneath a load of fear. In some cases, there is a gambling aspect to it; in others, where some definite obligation forces a man to face it, it represents the finest possible stimulant.

The protection of mankind from fear and terror doesn't imply the abolition of risk; it implies, on the contrary, the permanent presence of a certain amount of risk in all aspects of social life; for the absence of risk weakens courage to the point of leaving the soul, if the need should arise, without the slightest inner protection against fear. All that is wanted is for risk to offer itself under such conditions that it is not transformed into a sensation of fatality.

PRIVATE PROPERTY

Private property is a vital need of the soul. The soul feels isolated, lost, if it is not surrounded by objects which seem to it like an extension of the bodily members. All men have an invincible inclination to appropriate in their own minds anything which over a long, uninterrupted period they have used for their work, pleasure or the necessities of life. Thus, a gardener, after a certain time, feels that the garden belongs to him. But where the feeling of appropriation doesn't coincide with any legally recognized proprietorship, men are continually exposed to extremely painful spiritual wrenches.

Once we recognize private property to be a need, this implies for everyone the possibility of possessing something more than the articles of ordinary consumption.

The forms this need takes can vary considerably, depending on circumstances; but it is desirable that the majority of people should own their house and a little piece of land round it, and, whenever not technically impossible, the tools of their trade. Land and livestock figure among the tools necessary to the peasant's trade.

The principle of private property is violated where the land is worked by agricultural labourers and farm-hands under the orders of an estate-manager, and owned by townsmen who receive the profits. For of all those who are connected with that land, there is not one who, in one way or another, is not a stranger to it. It is wasted, not from the point of view of corn-production, but from that of the satisfaction of the property-need which it could procure.

Between this extreme case and that other one of the peasant who cultivates with his family the land he owns, there are a number of intermediate states where Man's need of appropriation is more or less unrecognized.

COLLECTIVE PROPERTY

Participation in collective possessions – a participation consisting not in any material enjoyment, but in a feeling of ownership – is a no less important need. It is more a question of a state of mind than of any legal formula. Where a real civic life exists, each one feels he has a personal ownership in the public monuments, gardens, ceremonial pomp and circumstance; and a display of sumptuousness, in which nearly all human beings seek fulfilment, is in this way placed within the reach of even the poorest. But it isn't just the State which ought to provide this satisfaction; it is every sort of collectivity in turn.

A great modern factory is a waste from the point of view of the need of property; for it is unable to provide either the workers, or the manager who is paid his salary by the board of directors, or the members of the board who never visit it, or the shareholders who are unaware of its existence, with the least satisfaction in connection with this need.

When methods of exchange and acquisition are such as to involve a waste of material and moral foods, it is time they were transformed.

There is no natural connection between property and money. The connection established nowadays is merely the result of a system which has made money the focus of all other possible motives. This system being an unhealthy one, we must bring about a dissociation in inverse order.

The true criterion in regard to property is that it is legitimate so long as it is real. Or, to be more precise, the laws concerning property are so much the better the more advantages they draw from the opportunities offered by the possessions of this world for the satisfaction of the property-need common to all men.

Consequently, the present modes of acquisition and possession require to be transformed in the name of the principle of property. Any form of possession which doesn't satisfy somebody's need of private or collective property can reasonably be regarded as useless.

That does not mean that it is necessary to transfer it to the State; but rather to try and turn it into some genuine form of property.

TRUTH

The need of truth is more sacred than any other need. Yet it is never mentioned. One feels afraid to read when once one has realized the quantity and the monstrousness of the material falsehoods shamelessly paraded, even in the books of the most reputable authors. Thereafter one reads as though one were drinking from a contaminated well.

There are men who work eight hours a day and make the immense effort of reading in the evenings so as to acquire knowledge. It is impossible for them to go and verify their sources in the big libraries. They have to take the book on trust. One has no right to give them spurious provender. What sense is there in pleading that authors act in good faith? *They* don't have to do physical labour for eight hours a day. Society provides for their sustenance so that they may have the leisure and give themselves the trouble to avoid error. A pointsman responsible for a train accident and pleading good faith would hardly be given a sympathetic hearing.

All the more reason why it is disgraceful to tolerate the existence of newspapers on which, as everybody knows, not one of the collaborators would be able to stop, unless he were prepared from time to time to tamper knowingly with the truth.

The public is suspicious of newspapers, but its suspicions don't save it. Knowing, in a general way, that a newspaper contains both true and false statements, it divides the news up into these two categories, but in a rough-and-ready fashion, in accordance with its own predilections. It is thus delivered over to error.

We all know that when journalism becomes indistinguishable from organized lying, it constitutes a crime. But we think it is a crime impossible to punish. What is there to stop the punishment of activities once they are recognized to be criminal ones? Where does this strange notion of non-punishable crimes come from? It constitutes one of the most monstrous deformations of the judicial spirit.

Isn't it high time it were proclaimed that every discernible crime is a punishable one, and that we are resolved, if given the opportunity, to punish all crimes?

A few straightforward measures of public salubrity would protect the population from offences against the truth.

The first would be to set up, with such protection in view, special courts enjoying the highest prestige, composed of judges specially selected and trained. They would be responsible for publicly condemning any avoidable error, and would be able to sentence to prison or hard labour for repeated commission of the offence, aggravated by proven dishonesty of intention.

For instance, a lover of Ancient Greece, reading in

one of Maritain's books: 'The greatest thinkers of antiquity had not thought of condemning slavery', would indict Maritain before one of these tribunals. He would take along with him the only important reference to slavery that has come down to us – the one from Aristotle. He would invite the judges to read the sentence: 'Some people assert that slavery is absolutely contrary to nature and reason.' He would observe that there is nothing to make us suppose these particular 'people' were not among the greatest thinkers of antiquity. The court would censure Maritain for having published – when it was so easy for him to avoid falling into such a mistake – a false assertion, and one constituting, however unintentionally, an outrageous calumny against an entire civilization. All the daily papers, weeklies and others, all the reviews and the radio would be obliged to bring the court's censure to the notice of the public, and, if need be, Maritain's answer. In this particular case, it seems most unlikely there could be one.

On the occasion when Gringoire, published *in extenso* a speech attributed to a Spanish anarchist, who had been announced as going to speak at a meeting in Paris, but who in fact, at the last minute, had been unable to leave Spain, a court of this kind would not have been out of place. Dishonesty being in such a case more patent than that two and two make four, no doubt prison or hard labour would not have been too severe a sentence.

Under this system, anybody, no matter who, discovering an avoidable error in a printed text or radio broadcast, would be entitled to bring an action before these courts.

The second measure would be to prohibit entirely all propaganda of whatever kind by the radio or daily press. These two instruments would only be allowed to be used for non-tendentious information.

The aforesaid courts would be there to see that the information supplied was not tendentious.

In the case of organs of information, they might have to pronounce judgment concerning not only erroneous assertions, but also intentional and tendentious omissions.

Circles in which ideas are discussed, and which desire to make them known, would only have a right to publish weekly, fortnightly or monthly journals. There is absolutely no need to appear more frequently in print, if one's object is to make people think instead of stupefying them.

The propriety of the methods of persuasion used would be guaranteed, thanks to the control exercised by the above courts, which would be able to suppress any publication guilty of too frequent a distortion of the truth; though the editors would be allowed to let it reappear under another name.

Nothing in all this would involve the slightest attack on public liberty. It would only mean satisfaction of the human soul's most sacred need – protection against suggestion and falsehood.

But, it will be objected, how can we guarantee the impartiality of the judges? The only guarantee, apart from that of their complete independence, is that they should be drawn from very different social circles; be naturally gifted with a wide, clear and exact intelligence; and be trained in a school where they receive not just a legal education, but above all a spiritual one, and only secondarily an intellectual one. They must become accustomed to love truth.

There is no possible chance of satisfying a people's need of truth, unless men can be found for this purpose who love truth.